Friends First

Claire Pedrick and Andy Morgan

ISBN 978 1 84427 503 8

Scripture Union
207–209 Queensway, Bletchley, Milton Keynes, MK2 2EB
Email: info@scriptureunion.org.uk
Website: www.scriptureunion.org.uk

Scripture Union Australia
Locked Bag 2, Central Coast Business Centre, NSW 2252
Website: www.scriptureunion.org.au

Scripture Union USA
PO Box 987, Valley Forge, PA 19482
Website: www.scriptureunion.org

Scripture quoted from the Contemporary English Version © American Bible Society
1991, 1992, 1995. Anglicisations © British and Foreign Bible Society 1996. Published
in the UK by HarperCollinsPublishers and used with permission.

British Library Cataloguing-in-Publication Data.
A catalogue record of this book is available from the British Library.

Printed and bound in India by Thomson Press.
Cover design by Martin Lore

Scripture Union is an international Christian charity working with churches in
more than 130 countries, providing resources to bring the good news about Jesus
Christ to children, young people and families and to encourage them to develop
spiritually through the Bible and prayer.

As well as our network of volunteers, staff and associates who run holidays, church-
based events and school Christian groups, we produce a wide range of publications
and support those who use our resources through training programmes.

Thanks to the support and inspiration of many who helped with the first edition – particularly R121: Oli, David, Rebecca, Ruth, Will and Ed for being willing to be open, honest and make us think! And to say what they really feel! Michael Stratford inspired the whole idea about teams that we explore throughout the book. Thanks to Mark Buchanan, Director of DPM-UK, whose seminar 'Bridging the Generations' was instrumental for the ideas in the 'Generations and Grannies' chapter.

Also, thank you to the adults who were also willing to say what they think: Diane Clutterbuck, Peter Meadows, Rosalind and Richard Nevard, Madeleine Nicholas and Anne Purcell.

For the second edition, we have been helped by Claire's teenagers – Lucy and Ellie.

Most of all thanks to our best friends, Mike and Kitty.

Contents

Contents

Note to parents

If you're reading this, is it because:
• you're thinking of buying it to give to your teenager?
• you like to know what your teenager is reading?
• you're unsure how to handle the whole relationships thing with them?

A few years ago, there was a TV documentary called *Mum, I'm a Muslim*. It followed the stories of four white British women who had converted to Islam. What they had in common was a desire for some definite rules and boundaries, and much of this related to wearing a Hijab. That's the scarf and clothing that tries to cover up the fact they're drop dead gorgeous and saves their looks for the men they will marry.

In the Christian church, the laws are less definite and our young people are caught in a tide between popular culture and confusion about what the Bible says about relationships. This also gets mixed up with what church culture says about what is and isn't OK.

The rate of change in culture is unsurpassed. Young people are more different than we can ever imagine. Theirs is an instant world. Many teenagers sleep with their mobiles on and may wake to respond to text messages. Facebook is a hub for chatting, dumping and making arrangements. If you were hungry you may have gone down the chip shop or for a kebab. They can phone food in or walk into fast food outlets for breakfast, lunch and dinner. You had to be in to see your favourite TV show or miss it! They can record it or watch it on the internet and there is pressure to broadcast or tweet every second of their lives online.

Parenting young people is a tough job. Congratulations on staying committed and wanting to be involved! You may feel out of your depth, especially if technology, texts and the web are something with which you feel uncomfortable. Nevertheless, it's important to spend time getting to know the culture of today. This may mean reading books on culture or watching TV you wouldn't normally watch! We've suggested some books you may like to look at on page 9.

Your teenager has been taking assessments at school since they were seven. They are doing external exams right through secondary school. In their instant culture, news can spread around the neighbourhood, the town and the world in seconds. They want an instant decision on those new trainers! They may have a strong questioning spirit. Why do I have to wait – for anything? This isn't just disobedience – it comes from the instant culture. How do you respond? Your answer may still be no… but how do you communicate that?

And then there's sex. It's not good enough just to say don't do it. In every song, TV show, magazine or book, sex is on the agenda in some way. Sex is even used to sell minis! Young people are not thinking about sex earlier than you might have because they're debauched! They are bombarded from every angle. They know the language of sex. People at school are doing it. There's pressure.

Your home needs to be a place away from the pressures. This might mean a place to chill out and sleep late at the weekends. They may not want to come to church on Sunday morning but you can still give them spiritual input and encourage them. Set aside time in your diary to spend time with your teenager. It may be going out, or just sitting and watching a DVD with a bowl of Ben & Jerry's.

In terms of our teenagers and romance, the only model we have to look at is the 'choosing a partner' model. Many churches and Christian leaders are very firm that you shouldn't go out with someone unless you would consider marrying them.

And that's absolutely right – if you're in your twenties. But what pressure if you're 13! What connection does marriage have with wanting to go out for a date? How do you know if you'd even want to marry someone? This paradigm creates enormous pressure and makes relationships exclusive when all that young people are doing is exploring what relationships are about. It is far more important for teenagers to be able to relate to others in many different ways. Maybe they will marry their first boyfriend or girlfriend. Maybe they won't. But for now, that's not even a question at all. Being friends is first.

'I want rules, but not too strict – like "Always tell me where you're going" – even if we go somewhere else! Give us some space. Take some time in the back seat. You don't have to always be in the driving seat all the time.'

'Don't always think the worst of me… or the best of me either! Don't put me in a box. Let me be a bit flexible. When you've sent me to jail, and I'm in my room waiting to throw a double six, be prepared to sell me a 'Get out of Jail Free' card. You're really cool, but I'm not going to tell you that!'

Suggested books for parents of young people
Essential Youth, Andy Hickford (Kingsway)
Generating Hope, Jimmy Long (HarperCollins)
Grove Booklet P76: *Postmodern Culture and Youth Discipleship – Commitment or Looking Cool?*, Graham Cray (Grove Booklets Ltd)
Youthwork and the mission of God, Pete Ward (SPCK)
The Path to Purpose, William Damon (Free Press)

Intro

start here

Love is… sex within minutes. Love is… woolly tights and acrylic jumpers

Is that all? Every day, we're bombarded with images on TV, the internet and in magazines and newspapers about relationships. They can be exciting, enthralling… and confusing. And what we see on TV may not fit with what we see at home or at church.

The world says, 'Anything goes', 'Do what you like'. The church says, 'Don't do it!', 'Be careful'. So how do you stop being torn apart? And are all relationships about going out and sex? What about other friends?

STOP! Rewind! Go back to basics. Let's put everything aside and look at what the Bible says about relationships. No assumptions. Let's cut the crap and face the facts…

You're human. Sex before marriage is wrong, but what do you do with all those feelings?

Do you get to 13 and have a temporary castration or wear a chastity suit and then emerge at 21 ready to face the world?!

You want to honour God and your friends are smoking dope, taking drugs or drinking. Do you walk away? Or stay in the crowd?

When your mum and dad were kids, their parents knew a lot more than they did about the world. Now you can find out virtually anything you want to know by surfing the web. Mum and Dad may know best, but you may know much more than they do about the rainforest, nuclear physics, downloading and texting! You probably entered puberty a few years earlier than your parents. The world is a new place. As a Christian, where do you fit in?

'You only get one shot at this, so be as wise as you can be with the years you've got.'
Dad

You're a whole person, and that means all your bits are important – your spiritual bit, your emotions, your body and your mind. To be a whole Christian, you need to look at all your bits. Spiritual knowledge alone makes for a rather wonky life! God is also totally interested in everything about you: your close relationships with boys, girls, parents, brothers and sisters and other significant people.

Jesus was a whole person. He was a single bloke with a close relationship with his mother; he picked up children, was friends with the prostitute, Mary Magdalene, allowed a bloke (Judas) to kiss him... and ate with undesirable people.

It's time to learn how to live in the world as a Christian. God stuff is totally important. And God has an opinion on everything!

(By the way, if you want your parents to have a different take on some of these questions why not leave *Friends First* lying around and make sure they pick it up?)

What makes a person whole or balanced? They know themselves. They know God.

They can befriend others without fear. They are not afraid of their weaknesses. They're willing to ask for help. And how do we make relationships? Keep them? Break them? How can relationships be fun, enjoyable and useful?

A question: if your life is a sports match, who else is in your team? Who are the players who bring in the sponsorship, the social life and the excitement? Which are the positions you need to fill – like the goalie and the centre half (having a fun friend, a friend to be miserable with or a learn-about-God-friend)? And who are the people who just have to be in the team, no matter what part they fill?

No one person can cover all the positions in your team. If we try to bring all things out in one person, we'll see failure and feel let down or offended. An exclusively two-person team also pushes other people out – whether that's boyfriend and girlfriend or joined-at-the-hip-best friends. And you may find that Auntie Val has a place in there, too!

The key to great friendships is to have a good team around you. Is Jesus in your team? And what's his position?

Brothers and sisters

My brother is SO irritating. He pesters me when I'm with my friends and teases me constantly at home. Sometimes I really hate him!

Relationships in families
Living closely together
Why do we find it hard to love people we're related to?

You can choose your friends but you can't choose your family! And brothers or sisters can drive us WILD. They can also be great friends. You're around your family much more than you are around anyone else. You've known them longer than almost anyone else.

'Even if we get on well there are times when I don't want to talk to him or look at him – he gets annoying.'

'My sister did confide in me something she couldn't tell Mum and Dad. That was cool.'

We don't have anything in common. What's the point?
You have plenty in common. You're in the same family! You have plenty of shared experiences. You're more alike than you think you are… and sometimes that's what makes

---

Five reasons why brothers and sisters are irritating!

1 They know exactly what to do to drive you CRAZY!
2 They'll tell M&D a totally different story about why that precious thing got broken.
3 They always eat the last Kit Kat.
4 They borrow your straighteners without asking.
5 You have to go on holiday with them.

your brother or sister quite SO IRRITATING! They could be your best mate – but you're just as likely to be at war! You see, you'd let your best mate borrow the straighteners, eat the last Kit Kat (or at least split it 50:50!), or come into your room. With your brothers and sisters, as you find out who you are, they can become a bit more like rivals and get in your way. So from having an open door to your bedroom, you suddenly say NO ONE can come in. But don't forget that you get in their way too!

Isn't it annoying that you get told off for stuff and your brother doesn't? Or at least that's how it feels. Everyone's different, and needs to be treated differently. If you're older and you're told you should know better, it's not fair. If you're younger and the others are allowed to do stuff that you're not, it's not fair!

'He got three degrees more pizza than me!'

Life's not fair. You're born in the order you are born in – God's sense of fun, humour or whatever! If you're older, you will have to take more responsibility and you will have to wait longer to get privileges. That's life. If

Bible bit

How do you think Jesus got on with his brothers and sisters? Have a look at John 7:2–8. It seems that Jesus' own brothers had a problem with him. They almost appear to be taunting him, 'Go on, come to the feast and go public with what you think.' Jesus does not give in to the pressure of his brothers, even though they didn't believe in him. And in Mark 3:21, there's no doubt that his family thought, 'He's out of his mind!' Has anyone in your family ever said that about you?!

you're younger, you will be at home a few years longer than brothers and sisters. And they'll be able to go to parties and pubs and drive before you. But that's life, too! What's totally unfair is to continually take out how fed up you feel about your position in the family on your brothers or sisters. After all, it's no one's fault at all.

'He thinks he's superior sometimes. When I try to tell him he's not, he just goes, "Uh huh".'

13

'I don't get it. When I was 13 I got £5 pocket money. He gets £10. I'm still waiting for the back payment!'

(By the way, if you feel that your brother or sister is pestering you beyond acceptable bro/sis stuff then seek help from an adult in your team. If they are doing something that would embarrass you or make you feel ashamed if someone else was in the room, then look for help straight away.)

'It hurts more because they know your weak spots and they jab their finger where they know it hurts.'

Bible bit

There's nothing new about fiery relationships! Jacob teamed up with his mum Rebekah and pretended to be his older brother, Esau, so that Dad would give him the special blessing saved for the oldest child. After many years, they sorted it out – but during that time, Jacob was always afraid of what Esau might do in revenge. Have a look at Genesis 25–33 for the full story. And two of Jesus' disciples, brothers James and John, were so stroppy that Jesus called them Sons of Thunder!

I'm being bullied at school. I hate it and it makes my life a misery.

How do you cope?
Why does it happen?
What happens when your friends turn into your bullies?

Bullying is trying to have control over someone who can't or won't fight back. In a word, it's about intimidation.

What's the point of knowing this? If you heard that a friend of yours was suddenly on drugs, or addicted to alcohol, you'd probably ask what the problem was in their personal life. What was going on at home? The same goes with bullies.

Their actions show that there's deeper stuff going on. This is no excuse, nor does it make it any easier to cope with as you have to face it, or experience it. But it's often the facts.

'I felt crap. You think you're a freak, and ask yourself, "Why are they doing it to me?" I didn't know why I was being bullied. I think it was because they could – they pick on the weakest one to make themselves look big.'

What should I do? Sock it to 'em? Turn the other cheek? Run away?

Why do you feel intimidated by bullies? Well, bullying affects your self-image. It makes you feel small. Bullies use a mixture of physical and verbal attacks. They might push you around or call you names. When someone does this, of course you believe that they are actually a threat to you physically. Or you believe what they say about you. Even if you haven't got a big nose, if a crowd of people keep saying you have, you'll begin to get a real thing about your nose!

If you've been bullied, you may well try to withdraw and keep it to yourself. That's totally normal. You may feel ashamed about the fact that you've been bullied. And your parents may often be the last to know. You might be afraid to tell anyone in case they make a fuss, which will just make it worse. Or you may think they'll give you a load of useless advice like, 'Ignore them' or, 'It won't last for ever'. If you try to talk to someone though, they may surprise you.

'They bully you because you're different – you're a geek, or you wear glasses, or you don't have a big bundle of friends around.'

We all want to be liked and accepted for who we are, and it hurts us deep inside when people don't like us and say unkind things about us. The old rhyme 'sticks and stones will break my bones but names will never hurt me' is the biggest lie on the planet. Of course names hurt us – and names can damage us. But they can only damage us if we let them. The reason why names hurt us is because we know they are true, they might be true, or they're nearly true. When I was at school I was bullied because I was overweight. And I was overweight. The reason it hurt was that people emphasised the very thing that was different about me. People are bullied because they study hard at school, or because they are spotty, or because they are small, or because they are a different colour. All of this is emphasising the very thing that makes them different from others.

Part of having a good self-image is knowing yourself and accepting who you are. You may be big, small, a different colour than most of your class, spotty, wear glasses or are very brainy but once you know that you are OK as you are, and more importantly, that God thinks you are great, then what people choose to try and say about you does not really matter. Also, it's very hard to physically intimidate a person who is confident in him or herself and has a good self-image – even if he/she is very short.

'It's the very fact that I know who I am that makes me stand out. This is something to celebrate! If you pay a bully a compliment, it can pay dividends! After all, "Smile! It confuses people"!'

If you are being physically bullied, it's OK to avoid the people if you can. It's not about being brave but about being sensible. Neither is it cowardly nor a sign of weakness. If you are being bullied at school, and it's not that easy to avoid the bullies, then why not take up a form of basic self-defence. Learn how to block a punch. This isn't so that you can sock it back to them… but so that if you know you can defend yourself, they'll sense that the fear is gone and are more likely to leave you alone. And if they don't, you can defend yourself, should you ever need to.

But if you are being bullied, you must tell someone on your team. Find someone you can trust and confide in them. It may be hard to do, and they may not be able to do anything about the person bullying you, but they can stand by you, pray with you so that you can discover God's acceptance of who you are, and look out for your needs.

Bible bit

Did you know that Jesus was bullied? He was bullied because he was different. He spoke with authority. He told the religious leaders that they were wrong, and claimed he was God. In all of the Gospels it says that the Pharisees (the religious leaders of the day) plotted to kill Jesus. And how did Jesus respond? Have a look at John 8:59 and John 11:53,54. Jesus' life was threatened and people picked up stones to throw at him – and he hid himself and walked away. Is Jesus weak and wimpy? No. He stood up for what he believed and he took many verbal insults. Cruel remarks and insults were never a problem for Jesus because he knew who he was, where he came from and where he was going.

And the disciples? Well, Jesus says to them in Luke 22:36, '…if you don't have a sword, [go] and buy one.' Why did he do that? Because travelling those days was dangerous. Bandits and robbers would hide and rob unsuspecting travellers miles from any town or from any people. Protecting yourself was a necessity. Now, we're not suggesting you should buy a knife and arm yourself. But there's nothing wrong with protecting yourself, be it by avoiding danger or by learning how to block a punch. If you can sense danger, try and find a safe place or a safe adult as soon as possible.

Dumping and dating

AT 4 SR ~Ac

My mate Jess has gone out with half the class. She's with one boy for a week or so and then moves on to the next one. Is that right?

Does she know them before they go out?
Is she doing anything wrong?
Why is Jess dumping them?
What's the point of Jess going out with these boys?

One of the problems with dating is that as soon as you are seen alone with a boy/girl, even if you're just talking or walking together, you are automatically seen as 'in a relationship' or 'boyfriend and girlfriend' and someone has updated their facebook status about you: 'Jez Taylor saw Jack out with Chloe – nice one, my son!' Even if you were only checking out the footie scores, your friends almost force this view, often with taunts such as, 'Oh, I saw you with Jack/Chloe – getting it on were you?!'

'It's a status thing: "I've got a girlfriend!"'

Baggage of going out

1 You feel pushed outside of your friendship group.
2 You might feel pressure to snog, touch and maybe even to have sex.
3 There may be a conflict between how much time to spend with your friends or your boy/girlfriend.
4 You could feel like you have to commit all your emotional feelings to this relationship and neglect your friends.

> **'Is there a difference between going out with your friends and going out with a girl? Why is one a date and the other not?'**

Does it matter what other people think?

The idea that two teenagers of the opposite sex can be friends is no longer accepted. Our culture says: Boy + Girl = Sex. If a girl shows the slightest interest in being friends with a boy, it's interpreted as a 'come on'. Why can't 'going out' be called 'friendship making' instead? Why call it 'going out' or 'dating'? If two girls or two boys went out to the cinema or to a party, people wouldn't call it a 'date'.

Let's get back to Jess and her situation. Maybe she's a friendly person who likes to be friends with boys, has fun with them, and enjoys their company. Yet once she is friends with a boy, down comes the pressure for the relationship to be something bigger than it actually is.

> **'A friendship group can be trashed because three of you get girlfriends and you don't see your friends after that.'**

So Jess calls the shots and then needs to ignore what other people say?

The big question is what's really the point of Jess going out with these boys? Maybe it's to find acceptance or get a bit of attention. It might be to get affection or simply to make friends.

Who are these blokes? Are they part of her friendship group, or boys she's never met before?

And then there are her friends! Maybe they are part of the problem! Are they making Jess' friendships with these guys more than they actually are? Is she dumping them… or is she putting the brakes on before it all goes too far? Or maybe her idea of a relationship is different from her friends' ideas?

> **'There's a certain level of commitment needed in being boyfriend and girlfriend.'**

'At a party, my friend got off with five boys in one night. Are they all her boyfriends now? She already had a boyfriend!'

And Jess will still have to be around them afterwards, especially if they're in the same school or youth group. We make 'going out' into something more than it should be. Friendship with people of the same and opposite sex is really important. One of the benefits of being in a peer group is that you can practise friendships. You learn how to handle disagreements, conflicts and relationships all within the safety of a friendship group. Peer groups should be a safe place in which to learn, grow and make mistakes. You will change and so will the way you deal with other people. So why must we automatically assume that a boy-girl couple are more than just friends?

'Boundaries?! If you talked about relationship boundaries, you'd get laughed at!'

'Be careful about pairing off with someone else in the group. It could affect the whole group.'
Minister

'There's a minimum level of commitment in going out together – like not looking at someone else and then asking them out!'

What does the Bible say about friendship?
Well, there's all the love your neighbour bits, don't spread rumours, and treat people nicely. In fact, the ninth commandment says that we shouldn't tell lies about our neighbour (in other words, anyone we come into contact with). We need to be careful what we say about our friends, especially when it's connected with other people. How we treat one another is very important to God. And that's the main issue about dating and dumping.

We can feel as though we have to invest all our emotions and feelings into a relationship when in fact we should merely be enjoying being friends. When that relationship eventually comes to an 'end', instead of remaining friends and just continuing as part of the peer group, one person gets 'dumped', which feels like a massive rejection. And we all know how it feels to be rejected. It hurts and it can mess us up. God calls us to honour people, not to reject them. He calls us to look out for other people's feelings and not to hurt them. 'Don't be jealous or proud, but be humble and consider others more important than yourselves. Care about them as much as you care about yourselves' (Philippians 2:3,4).

'If you do go into a relationship with a boy or girl, don't get too exclusive. It's unreal. Include your parents and others in your friendship.' Dad

'Being dumped causes confusion, anger, and insecurity.'

'Investing emotions and sharing so much leads to animosity between you when it ends.'

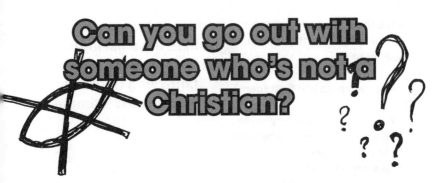

Can you go out with someone who's not a Christian?

I really fancy this girl at school. She's not a Christian. Help! What do I do?

All the Christian boys I know are wimps. Help!

First of all, rewind! Remember what this dating stuff is about. It's about being friends first and not being exclusive. So in one way there's no problem.

> 'What kind of relationship is it? Physical? When do you say you are definitely going out with someone?'

What might be the issues of going out with someone who's not a Christian?
Would you want to go out with someone who was really interested and involved in something you weren't? Like tae kwon do… or being a cheerleader?

Well – you might get interested in what they're doing… or you might start persuading them to spend more time with you and quit their other interests… or if you are a patient and open-minded person, you might just let them get on with it!

> 'It's not one of these things which people talk about unless they're really heavy people.'

So if you decide it's OK to go out with someone who's not a Christian, there are some things to just keep switched on at the back of your mind:

• If your idea is to be friends first and have some fun, is that theirs, too? Have they been out with loads of people?

23

• Are they going to want to go further physically than you are willing to go?

• How much do you trust them?

• What will you do if they begin to pull you away from what you believe? How will you notice that's happening?

'You've got to be friends first before you go out with someone.'

When you get older, there are loads of practical reasons why marrying someone who isn't a Christian can be difficult. Here are just a couple:

• Your focus is on being a Christian and following Jesus as well as being in a relationship with them. They won't be able to share what's basically the biggest part of your life. And you could feel yourself being pulled in two different directions.

• You may be living life by different rules and have different attitudes to money, work, family etc.

'It's hard when you can't share the most intimate part of your life (your faith) with the person you're most intimate with.'

And although there's a huge difference between dating and marrying, some people do marry their first date. Going out with someone who is not a Christian doesn't taint you or make you awful – but it does make everything a whole load less simple.

There's nothing in the Bible that says you can only spend time with people who are just like you. It's good to mix with lots of different people and they will learn more about your friends – including Jesus. In fact, Paul even tells us to make friends with the immoral people of this world (1 Corinthians 5:10). Jesus hung out with all kinds of people, and even with a former prostitute called Mary. If a Christian girl and a non-Christian boy developed a friendship, which involved them going (with other friends) to the cinema or Pizza Hut, the Christian girl is likely to receive pressure from either her parents, her church leader, her youth minister, or in the worst case, all of them, about the relationship. This immediately makes something more of the friendship than there is, and can cause more damage than good.

Some helpful advice from the Bible comes in Matthew 22:37–39. Jesus says, 'Love the Lord your God with all your heart, soul, and mind… love others as much as you love yourself'. This means your boy/girlfriend doesn't come first, which would be hard for someone who doesn't understand why. In the end, we have to be responsible for our own decisions. And we're responsible for our side of our relationship with God. What is more important to you? A relationship with a boy/girl or a relationship with God? Who has more influence in your life? A boy/girl or God? Only you can answer these questions.

'We must keep our eyes on Jesus.'
Hebrews 12:2

And by the way, the same rules apply with a non-Christian friend as with a Christian friend – don't be alone in a house, or start kissing and touching while there's absolutely no one around or coming back soon.

'Remember that if you're going to take a relationship beyond friendship, it's good if the other person's a Christian. Who knows how serious you'll get, and if they're not a Christian it will be hard to ask the question "Is this right?" once you are very involved.'
Mum

If you're not going out with a non-Christian, don't go looking for a relationship with one! If you are, then the number one thing is to be sure that you stay close to Jesus.

Whoever you go out with, there are two keys in a relationship. One is trust. The other is being clear about what you believe is acceptable or not and sticking to it whatever you are told by a boy/girl. Listen to this:

'After going out with lovely non-Christians I became a Christian and went out with a Christian guy who had just come back to faith. The first date we had it snowed and he had to stay the night. He told me that as long as two people love each other it's OK to sleep together because it's not a sin. I lost my virginity. It was only in the morning that I realised what had happened and that he'd made me do something I'd been really determined I wouldn't do. You see I believed him. No matter who you are having a relationship with, you really need to know them because even Christians can use God as an excuse to get their own way. Just because they have a Christian label stuck to them does not make them safe or mean that their relationship with God is OK.'

Can't pull, won't pull

My sister isn't interested in boys and her friends say there's nothing wrong with it. I'm not interested in girls and my friends say I'm gay.

issues

Is it all right not to be interested in the opposite sex? **What** does our culture say? **Is** it more about image than fact?

What is the problem?

The problem is that growing up today is tough, especially where relationships are concerned. Unfortunately our culture has two pigeonholes for teenage boys – those who are able to 'pull' girls and those who are seen as gay. Often if you reach 15 or 16 and you've never had a girlfriend you're seen as odd at best or labelled gay at worst. Usually such taunts are cruel ways of bullying. But it does underline a deeper issue. Is it acceptable to simply not be interested in the opposite sex?

'There's more pressure on you at 13 and 14 to go out with a girl because all your friends are going out with girls. There's more people breaking away from friendship groups and going out with girls for the first time... and they think they're better than you.'

Bible bit

Jesus never had a girlfriend. Was he gay? No. Was he a loser? No. Actually he was the toughest person ever to walk this planet. He took on his shoulders everything you and me have ever done wrong and then took on the devil and trounced him.

Where do all these ideas come from, anyway?

'Testosterone is more powerful than oestrogen – animal instinct.'

A lot of these ideas have come from movies. James Bond – and almost every other action hero – has influenced our culture. The guy always gets the girl. And it's not just any old guy – it's either the action hero guy, the vulnerable guy who does something heroic, or it's the weedy guy who becomes strong and proves he's a real man. And often they're in bed within minutes! Is that real life?

Of course not! The media feeds us these ideas all the time. Just look at *Friends* – a great TV story of a group of friends living in New York. Right from the very start, we had the chemistry between Ross and Rachel, but it didn't end there. The writers brought Monica and Chandler together and even had innuendos between Joey and Phoebe. They couldn't have the gang stay just friends with each other. In fact, Chandler often has 'gay' jokes made about him, mainly because of his lack of girl success (before Monica).

Yet Chandler ends up the most successful of the group in terms of a happy relationship.

'I actually find Chandler more attractive than the other men in *Friends*. I guess it's because he's sensitive and understands himself – that's really important'

What would happen in a movie if the tough guy turned to the attractive heroine and said, 'Hey, actually, I'm not really interested in a relationship with you, or with any other girl for that matter. I'm not that attracted to girls.' He would be seen as weird!

There's an old film called *When Harry Met Sally* with Billy Crystal and Meg Ryan. Harry tells Sally that it's impossible for a guy to be just friends with a girl. He tries to come on to Sally, who tells him that they will only ever be friends. Harry responds by saying, 'We can never be friends. Men and women can't be friends because the sex part gets in the way… no man can be friends with a woman who is attractive.'

But that isn't true! You can just be friends.

So what can I do?

Look around at school. Is everybody going out with someone? NO! Your life isn't substandard because you don't have a boy/girlfriend. Just enjoy being who you are. Simply not having a boyfriend or girlfriend does not mean you're gay! Neither does having friends who are the same sex as you. Many people who are in relationships take up a huge amount of the limelight at school. If you actually look around, there are a whole load of really pretty girls, and good-looking boys, who've NEVER been in a relationship in school.

So what's the difference between people like me and people who don't get hassled?

The problem is about image – what you look like and what image you project. The issue is not always about having a girlfriend. You can find two teenage boys, both who have never had a girlfriend, and one will be 'cool' while the other is labelled 'queer'. How come? It all comes down to the perception of whether you have the potential to pull. One might be athletic and relatively good-looking and most importantly, part of the in crowd, and this image means

Bible bit

Have a read of 1 Samuel 18–20. It tells the story of a friendship between David (who was to become King David) and Jonathan (son of King Saul). They became so close that four times it says that Jonathan loved David as himself. They were close friends. Not gay, just close friends.

he could get a girlfriend. This is regardless of whether he could actually get a girlfriend. He may have a personality of a one-cell amoeba, bad breath and smelly feet and any girl would dump him within 30 seconds of going out with him. But he has the right image. Yet if the other boy is skinny (or fat), may not yet be that good-looking, has spots and wears glasses he is deemed incapable of getting a girlfriend. This is regardless of whether he has a fun personality and a caring nature and that any girl who did go out with him would totally fall for him. And it's just the same for girls – the one with a Wonderbra and the one with a vest.

'If you hang around the cool guy with a girlfriend, even if you've never had one yourself, you're cool by default.'

Look at those people who aren't hassled for not having a girlfriend. They use the language, are quite confident, are seen around girls and join in with the group. It's crazy that when you're 9 you're seen as 'gay' for going around with girls. And by 15, you're gay because you don't!

As we've said, don't worry about not having a girlfriend. You're not incomplete without one... but you are incomplete if you can't relate to them at all... and

Bible bit

Jesus was someone who could relate to women. He had a close relationship with his mum. He had women travelling with him, including Mary Magdalene. What Jesus could do, perfectly, was to relate to both men and women.

Bible bit

Jesus was not afraid to say to a man, 'I love you'. Not because he was gay, but because he was able to be a true human being. John 21 has Jesus asking Peter three times, 'Do you love me?'

so is your sister if she can't relate to boys!

What next?
God's best is for us to be able to relate to anyone. So be friends first. Boys, be friends with girls. Girls, be friends with guys. Go out together in a group. Guys, girls are human beings! They're not:
• weird
• for pulling
• frightening

'Otherwise it's about being a shallow machine – me man + you woman = babies.'

Kissy Kissy

'Have rich friendships. Find a group of friends who do things together. Focus on your peer group rather than individuals. I hope that the church is providing a good focus for your meeting together and that this gives you a chance to have fun together outside Sundays, too. What do you all want to get out of being together? What have you to give to one another? How do you do that to include everyone?'
Minister

Part of the deal of growing up and becoming a fully matured (not in age) human being is that you grow spiritually, emotionally, physically, intellectually and SOCIALLY. How a boy interacts with a girl and a girl interacts with a boy is all part of your growing and maturing. And the best place to learn is in a safe 'friends' environment, not just by having a 'girlfriend'.

Bible bit

And in 1 Corinthians 7, Paul clearly talks about singleness being a good thing. It is not in competition with marriage – but an equally good and valid lifestyle.

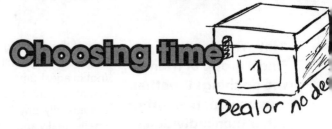

Dealor no deal

Choosing time

We've been going out for six months and it's great. We want to get engaged, but our parents say it's too early.

issues

How do you choose?
When do you know?

It's an exciting thing to have found someone who you enjoy being with. You just seem to click, and the time you spend together is wonderful. You can't wait for the next time you see each other. You just know that it will never end...

Just because you work for Tesco or Sainsbury's or have a Saturday job does not automatically mean that you will work in that job for the rest of your life. Just because you live in London, or Letchworth, or Los Angeles does not mean you will always live there. Now, it may

turn out that you do live in the same place for life, or work in the same job all your life – and that's OK. In the same way, just because you are going out with someone who you really like does not mean you will end up marrying them. You could end up marrying them, but it doesn't mean you have to or that you will.

'Every time I went out with a boy I thought – could he be the one?'

Surely I've got to make a choice sometime?
Yes, you will make a choice one day, but it will be a choice based on more than just the fact that you like someone and get on with him or her. Also, the issue is not that you shouldn't make a choice NOW, but that you don't need to.

You could – and some people do – choose all the subjects you will study for your GCSEs by the time you are 12. But you're not asked to sign a piece of paper at 12 to finalise the subjects you will do!

You make that decision later. With your boyfriend/girlfriend, you could make the decision that you will marry them now, but you don't have to make that choice now.

We can take great care over which mobile to buy, or which iPod to have, or which clothes to look good in. We often spend a long time thinking what would be best. We need to take even more care over the choice of our future partner (or whether you want to have a partner at all – not everyone HAS to get married).

'Life is about making the right decisions and living with the consequences.'
Dad

Bad choices don't just go away! God is a great God, and when we love him, he NEVER holds

Bible bit

Poor old Samson. He had a habit of making quick decisions. If you want to read about it, check out Judges 14 – 16. Samson sees a woman he likes, goes home and tells his parents, 'Get her for me!' His parents aren't too happy, but Samson marries her and it doesn't turn out well. Then he meets Delilah, marries her and that goes a bit pear-shaped, too. Samson had loads of things going for him, but he did rush his decisions.

our bad choices against us. However, we do have to work through our bad choices. That isn't often easy, although God helps us loads.

'You go out because it's fun.'

So how will I ever know when to choose?

One way is to look at the Bible in 1 Corinthians 13. You may feel that you love the person you are with. Let's test it out. Is your love for your boy/girlfriend:

• patient
• kind
• free from jealousy
• free from boasting
• free from pride
• free from rudeness
• never demanding your own way
• free from being irritable and grumpy
• never holding anything against them – no blame
• free from injustice
• always loving the truth
• always going to continue and never give up
• going to endure through EVERY circumstance?

Wow – what a list. If you can agree with all of this, then you are well on the way to choosing.

But usually it takes a while to get to this point.

And by the way, girls are you willing to do anything for your boyfriend? And hey, boys are you willing to die for your girlfriend? That's another condition of choosing your partner (Ephesians 5:24–26).

All of this doesn't necessarily mean that you can't end up marrying your boy/girlfriend who you have known since you were a teenager.

But now isn't the choosing time for you. You are still growing, developing and changing. Your hopes and dreams and expectations will change and grow with you. The deep feelings you develop for people are real feelings, but not necessarily the feelings that will help you choose when to get married.

What about my parents?

You know that your parents love you. They only want what's best for you, and you need to recognise that. But their job is also to love you unconditionally, even when you make bad choices. It's a good idea to listen to your parents. They may not always be right, and they may not know everything, but they have wisdom and experience that you can draw from. So use it.

'Adults put pressure on us to have adult kinds of relationships. All you really want to do is hang out.'

'I met this girl on holiday in the summer. We got on really well. I can't stop thinking about her. She lives 200 miles away so it's tough because we can only text and call and talk online.'
You can collect a lot of feelings when you meet someone for just a few days. The question is – what do you do with them?

Friendships can survive any distance. Texting, facebook and email have really helped. Even if someone is abroad, you can catch up on all the mindless news as well as all the significant stuff. Intimacy is more difficult – even if it's not physical. Just being around our friends creates an intimacy that can't be cloned by electronic wizardry.

Be friends first – remember? Carrying on a long distance relationship takes it away from being something that happens in a community. And hey – look

– here comes the PRESSURE!

Right through from your first hair to your last spot, you're changing. As your body changes, so does your life and lifestyle, and your beliefs, attitudes and feelings. That's a massive amount to handle long distance.

So long distance friends are fab. But think twice before you carry on something more serious.

'I was having a fun relationship but then my mum shouted him out because he was older and told him that he couldn't sleep with me. It was really awful – she said something that I hadn't even thought about.'

Church

My friends don't go to church. All the stuff I do is outside. Is that OK?

Friends at church
Expanding your team

It's great to have friends who don't go to church. It's also important to have some who do! If you're a Christian, your belief is as much a part of who you are as the colour of your skin, your family life and what you look like! Some of the time you need to be with other Christians and listen to them. You also need to listen to God through prayer and reading the Bible. Believing solo is really tough. It's like being a tenpin bowling player when everyone else plays netball or rugby. Going bowling on your own doesn't quite have the same feeling as going with friends, and imagine the way your style would change if you picked up tips from the playing field! Would you start tackling the player in the next lane? Finding a group of people who also do tenpin bowling would mean you could practise, learn more about it and most importantly enjoy it! And then you could see your netball or rugby friends after their match!

And the church needs you as much as you need the people there. Maybe you're in a place where there are very few young people. You still need each other! The church is not perfect.

Bible bit

Hebrews 10:25 says that Christians should not give up meeting together, but encourage one another. It's great being around people who care about you, accept you for who you are and who would help you out of tough situations. That's what church should be doing.

But what family is perfect? Every family has some problems from time to time and the church is no different from any other family. But it is based on Jesus' model. And although it has loads of faults, frustrations and annoying traditions, Jesus has promised to come back for the church and make it perfect. It is important for you to have church people in your team. There are always going to be times when you're looking for a bit of support – someone to encourage you or pray for you. And whatever you are going through, there will be someone somewhere who has been through it before. In the church we find an extra family. And it can be as important as the one at home!

'Older people can be cool, especially those whose children have just left home.'

You may think that your church is rubbish and doesn't do anything for young people. Even then, it's still important to be part of the church family in some way. The church needs to understand young people, but they're not going to do that if you've gone! You need to educate the church on how to

Bible bit

Have a look at Matthew 12:46–50. Church is supposed to be much more than just an hour-long meeting at some unearthly early hour on a Sunday morning. It's meant to be a family. Jesus is sitting with a load of people and his family show up for a chat. Someone says, 'Hey Jesus, your family is here.' Jesus says, 'Anyone who obeys my Father in heaven is my brother or sister or mother.' Now, Jesus isn't running down his family or disrespecting them. He uses this to teach the group something important – those who do the things God tells them to do are part of a huge family, and not just any old family, but part of Jesus' family – the Church.

understand and read the world in which you live. Similarly, you need to try and understand them; the world from which they have come, and the language they speak. It's back to different languages and cultures again. You may need to learn a bit about theirs just as they need to learn a bit about yours!

If you're really struggling and feel there's nothing in your church for young people, why not keep going there on a Sunday but look around for activities for Christian young people to go to at other times? You can actively seek out other Christian young people where you live. Look at Guide to Good Friends (page 54) to check out some places to start.

So your local church is a great place to find other adults to add to your team. There will be parents you can borrow! Who do you have in your team who you could go to in a crisis? It may well be the parents of one of your friends. Even Lucy in *EastEnders* has an adult she can trust somewhere. You may not know who your trusted adult might be right now, but it's good to get to know a variety of people so you have someone to turn to. You don't always want to go to your parents first. A mentor can be invaluable.

Bible bit

Have a read of Acts 2:43–47 and Acts 4:32–37. After Jesus had gone back home to heaven, the first believers relied on each other. They sold their possessions and they spent time together both at the temple (where they prayed to God) and in each other's homes, sharing meals. They relied on each other, supported each other and encouraged one other just like a family. Now you don't necessarily need to sell all your possessions, but a big part of your church family's job is to support, help and encourage you.

Crushes

she loves me she loves me not

I really fancy the boy who leads the Christian group at school. What should I do?

Are crushes good or bad?
Should you act on a crush?

Nice feeling, isn't it? Crushes happen, whatever age you are. Whether it's the bus driver, a leader or teacher, experiencing feelings for someone else is normal. It's part of growing up; it's part of life. Bet your mum has had a crush on someone!

'It's really embarrassing. Every time I see him I go, "Errrrrrr...". I think about him quite often... well, in every lesson!'

The exciting thing about crushes is that feeling you get when you see the person you like. Your heart starts beating faster, you get short of breath, and maybe your palms get sweaty. Your emotions start to take over.

And crushes can be harmless – as long as you recognise that they're just a bit of fun. The risk

Bible bit

King David's emotions took over quite dramatically. You can read all about it in 2 Samuel 11. While walking on the flat roof of his palace one day he saw Bathsheba in the bath. He fancied her straight away. PHWARGH! What a woman! However, his feelings led to thoughts, and his thoughts led to action. Even though David knew that Bathsheba was married, he had an affair with her. Eventually, David had her husband killed to hide the affair. OK, it's an extreme example. But it's hard to control our emotions sometimes.

Recognising a crush
- You're sending someone you don't know well more than a couple of texts a day and then staring at your mobile waiting for the reply.
- You find yourself thinking about them all through the day.
- Getting soppy!
- You wake up in the morning cuddling and kissing your pillow!
- You constantly check facebook

is not recognising that it's just a crush. When this happens, your emotions can take over, and this isn't always a good thing!

Crushes can be great. They often happen with people we respect or admire, and something about their magnificent fantabulous personality (or body) just makes us go 'Wooooooooooow!'

And often, crushes are with people we see but don't know, or at least, know only from a distance. Part of the crush is that we want to know the person better, to be more intimate with them. We see them in the distance and imagine them kissing us passionately, or just being your girl/boyfriend. And often it's not a sexual thing. Maybe someone affirms you, encourages you or just pays you some attention and you really like it.

The problem with crushes is that they're a mixture of reality and imagination. You see someone you like, and then you think of what it WOULD be like to be closer to him or her.

'Your mind substitutes your ideal fantasy for what you don't know about people.'

Sadly, crushes are often destroyed when you actually get closer to the person you like. You notice that their voice isn't deep and masculine (if they're a bloke), or high and sweet (if a girl) but annoyingly high-pitched and with a slight accent, or maybe they have acne, fart in public, pick their nose, or are even just plain boring. The point is nobody is as good as we can imagine him or her. And that's OK. But crushes become a problem when you become obsessed with a person, ignoring their faults and putting them on a pedestal of perfection.

'My friend had a crush on our teacher – she would send her letters, buy her presents... until the teacher had to tell her to back off. She's not a lesbian... she just got obsessive.'

'I talked to him and he was SO boring!'

So, are crushes bad?

'Depends on whether you start stalking...!'

Crushes aren't bad. They're a part of life, but they can become a problem when we let our emotions take over. Crushes are part of the process of discovering what we like and dislike in the opposite sex. Not just physically (brunette not blonde, short not tall etc) but in personality. So ask yourself, 'What do I find attractive about this person?', 'What don't I like about them?', 'Is there anything I can learn from them?' And crushes tell us we're still alive!

'Now I know I like brunettes...'

One thing you need to know is that a crush is not love. It's not even pre-love. The danger, and often the problem, is that we confuse a crush and love. That's not to say that you couldn't eventually fall in love with a person you had a crush on – but love and a crush are miles apart.

If a crush is a mixture of reality and imagination, then love is the acceptance of the reality in a person.

The difference between crushes and love
Look at 1 Corinthians 13 again. It doesn't say crushes are patient and kind, don't envy, don't boast etc. That's because crushes can be envious, they can be rude, and they can be impatient. But love is something far deeper than a crush. When you look at a person and say, 'Cor, I really fancy them!' are you thinking about marriage? A long-term commitment, parenthood, or looking after them when they are ill? No. That comes when you fall in love. Crushes come and crushes go!

My friend flirts with all these boys without any intention of going out with them, but I fancy one of them and I'm too embarrassed to say anything.

What is flirting?
Is there anything wrong with flirting?
Is it harmless fun?

'Flirting is about testing the water!'

'When a girl looks at you, it's a good sign. When she looks away, embarrassed, but then looks back, you know you're in.'

What is flirting?

According to one dictionary, flirting is a 'light-hearted and short-lived amorous attachment' or 'encouraging another's attention for amusement.' Actually, we flirt all the time. When you're asking your dad for £10 because you want to go out, and you look at him with BIG eyes, that's flirting! Your granny might be flirting when she's ordering a meal and is chatting to the waiter! When you tease for good fun that might be flirting, too. What we're talking about here, though, is flirting as a way of trying to get the attention of someone you fancy! At best, it's a way of getting someone to notice you. At worst, it's trying to make a fool of them. You know when peacocks show their amazing plume of feathers? That's flirting: 'LOOK AT ME! Aren't I gorgeous?!' Most animals have mating calls. 'Here I am, boys – let's be having you!' The difference between animals and people is that people are more complicated – it's called feelings!

So for us humans, what is flirting? Basically it's a way of testing the water to see whether someone likes you or not. You look. You smile. You raise your eyebrows. Or you say something, or maybe ask a searching question, hoping for a reply. If you get a response – a look or a comment – this gives you a kind of permission to ask another question. Eventually you can ask the real question – will you go out with me? That is, of course, if the flirting is for real. Sometimes it all turns into a joke for one person and massive embarrassment for the other.

Flirting is also about body language: touching, even blinking. Search the web for flirting and you'll get nearly 8 million results! Add to that the books, TV programmes and even weekend courses all telling you how to flirt. Most are very unhelpful! Flirting's really about confidence, knowing how far to take it and being aware if the other person is happy with what's going on.

'It's not what you say, but how you say it. With the internet and text, you read instead of hearing things. So, 'How're you doing', can be said in SO many ways... with so many meanings. It's even worse when you send the message to the wrong person. I once wrote 'Hey gorgeous' and put 'I love you' at the end of a text to Charlie (girl), but sent it to Charlie (boy)! He was a little bemused...'

So, what's the problem?
Where's the dividing line between flirting being OK and not being OK?

Flirting is about going beyond the way you'd just talk to a friend. It's about testing out how far you can go. The problem with flirting is that because you're pushing, there may be

Bible bit

When we get involved with relationships with other people, on whatever level, we need to remember how we should treat the other person. God asks us to treat one another with respect, honour and truth. 'Love your neighbour (in other words, anyone you know or see) as yourself.'

no clear edge. It can easily get out of control and you can find yourself in a situation that you don't know how to handle. It's not just about what you mean when you say and do certain things. It's about what the person you're with thinks you mean!

'You could flirt madly and the other person has no idea…'

'It's not always conscious.'

Flirting has taken a new turn with the web and texting. In chat rooms, you can flirt without people knowing who you are or where you live, so you can boldly say things that you would never say to someone you know, or who knew it was you saying it.

'Flirting through texting means it's easier to get the wrong end of the stick. You can read it again and again, reading different things into it.'

UR GR8 I WNT 2 CU 2NITE

Flirting through texting or facebook is even more risky. Again, it can easily go way beyond the normal way you would text a friend. And the person reading it can make it mean ANYTHING! As you're not face-to-face, you can end up texting things that you would never say if you were actually

---

What's good about flirting in a friendship group?
1 Bonding.
2 Practice – you can learn to judge when enough's enough.
3 You are unlikely to get extreme reactions.
4 There are always friends around to help settle hassle!

> **What happens if you fancy your youth leader?**
> 1 Flirting with your youth leader can make life difficult for them, and also for others in your group.
> 2 It will happen: most youth workers are meant to be role models. Attraction may simply turn out to be a feeling of 'I want to be like you when I'm older'.
> 3 Know that it's only fun. If it's more than that for you – stop it!
> 4 Look for the bits you find attractive in them in other people!

with them. Texting assumes that you know the person (unlike chat rooms) and at some point you will come face-to-face with them. Imagine coming face-to-face with a person after you've sent personal and intimate suggestions to them in a text or on facebook – even if it was just for a laugh. This can lead to trouble, misunderstandings and even harassment.

Are we saying flirting can be dangerous?
Flirting can be fun. And flirting can be dangerous. Playing with people's emotions can backfire, especially when you don't know them or have only met them briefly at a party. Look at *Big Brother*, *I'm a Celebrity* and all those reality shows – we watch people 24/7 just to see how far their flirting will go! (Yes, we do – would you watch it if they were only knitting a large blanket for Save the Children?)

'Flirting can bring out people's worst side.'

'Never flirt with someone who's got a boyfriend who is 6 foot 6.'

You may have no intention of going out with someone. But the person you are flirting with doesn't know this. Your flirting may well set off real and deep emotions in them. If you think that someone is interested in you but then you get rejected, this hurts your feelings. Sometimes it can cause real and deep hurt. And sometimes hurt can be visibly shown in anger, violence and in extreme cases, stalking.

'Some people are emotionally unstable. If you don't know them, then you don't know how they might react.'

So is flirting an absolute no-no? As we have discovered, we learn by doing stuff – in a safe peer group environment.
Flirting can be good, if it's done within a safe and trusting environment, with people whom you know who will not take advantage of you. Flirting is about trying things out. It's about asking questions like: Am I attractive to boys/girls? What happens if I use this look? When this is done in a peer group relationship, where you know the people well and trust them, then flirting can be part of growing into a complete person.

Grannies and generations

Want a Werthers Original dearie?

My gran wants me to come round and spend time with her. She's trying to be my friend. But she doesn't understand me!

issues

Can you be friends with grannies and other older people?

Whatever you do, don't treat your granny like an alien! Who cares if she wears really old-fashioned clothes (or just clothes that are ten years out of date!)? Who cares if her attitudes are rubbish and she doesn't like your hair products? If you can be friends with older people, there's loads to learn from them. And it can be fun! Maybe you speak different languages. But if you're willing to learn French or German or Japanese to get on in the world, why not learn to understand your gran? And while you're at it, get to know a few other older people.

The problem

Generations are not cooperating. Instead of mutual trust and respect we have suspicion and fear between generations. The world has changed more quickly in the last 30 years than at any other point in history. Your childhood and teenage years look nothing like your parents' or your grandparents'. Your grandparents were NEVER 'teenagers'. You've grown up with change and technology and you're used to it. You've never known a time without MP3s, computers, DVDs or mobiles, but your parents and grandparents have.

'I was walking down the high street. A group of elderly people were walking towards me. They looked afraid. In fact, I was terrified by them!'

It's really important to have an older person in your team. They'll often mediate between you and your parents. They love you – but they're a little bit removed from the hothouse of feelings between you and Mum and Dad!

'The reason grandparents and grandchildren get along so well is that they have a common enemy.'
Sam Levenson

The first thing you need to understand is that you and your gran – and other people of her generation – speak different languages. There's a huge gap between you and old people – a gap of years, culture and a society that is changing quicker than at any other point in history.

Bible bit

Psalm 145:4: 'Each generation will announce to the next your wonderful and powerful deeds.' Every generation thinks they know better than the last one and that there is nothing the 'oldies' can teach them. Actually, each generation passes on to the next the amazing things God has done and is doing. That means that you need to find out what God has done in the past and instead of ignoring it, you need to build on it. And then you can declare to YOUR children what God has done for you so they in turn can take it and build on it.

'One grandma is really old-fashioned: speak when you're spoken to! My other gran makes me cake and biccies while me and Grandad talk for hours about the rugby.'

'They'll talk to you about parent sort of things.'

loads to teach you. Unless they are a silver surfer, they may not know much about MP3 or texting or surfing the web, but they have experienced at least double the life that you have. This means that they can help you as you experience for the first time things that they have already experienced and lived through – and that can be really helpful!

'It's like networking Windows XP to Vista.'

'Some people lose their inhibitions after 60 and you can talk to them about anything – even sex. It's amazing!'

The gap is not impassable and if you can work out how to cross it, your gran could become one of your best and most useful friends.

You may not think it's true right now, but your parents, grandparents, aunts, teachers, and the elderly in your church and your neighbourhood have

You have to want to learn from your granny, or your parents. That means spending some

---

Why grannies are valuable friends!
• They've been around – and can relate to you better than you think.
• They are experienced – they know more than you think.
• They are understanding – they are more 'with it' than you think.
• They have years of wisdom – they can make sense of difficult situations better than you think.
• 'I'm friends with my grandma on facebook!'
You have a store of experience, wisdom and understanding in your grans – USE IT!

Bible bit

Leviticus 19:33,34 says: 'Don't ill-treat any foreigners who live in your land. Instead, treat them as well as you treat citizens and love them as much as you love yourself.'

The definition of a foreigner is someone who has no place in the culture. They don't have to be from another country! Not belonging can make you feel rejected, angry and frustrated. You may feel as though you don't belong. So can older people. The Bible says we are not to make people feel like they don't belong or to treat people like foreigners. It's a two-way street. And it's not only old and young. Our culture often tries to separate:
• men and women
• parents and children
• people and God
• young and old
• rich and poor

time listening to them. But it also means asking questions. Don't be afraid. What might be freaking you out now is almost certainly something that once freaked them out as well. Your older relatives and the elderly people in your church have been bullied, had crushes, fallen out with friends, been a Christian in the world, been in love, seen your parents make mistakes… and they have plenty to share with you! Older people can be energised by the passion, enthusiasm and ability of your generation. And they can make an investment in you and your friends – educationally, emotionally, financially and spiritually.

'Old ladies in hats? I want one of their hats – they're funky!'

You are physically bigger than your grandparents' generation. And if you like being with your friends, you'll go around with them. That can be quite scary for older people.

'Most of our friends are 15 and would think we are weird if we had friends who were old people.'

Top 10 reasons to be friends with old people:
• Gratitude and respect – after all if they've lived through a war they must be really grateful.
• They can teach you to dance, history and things.
• They can be real cracking fun!
• They say things your parents wouldn't.
• They can give you advice on life experience because they've done it.
• They are well knowledgeable.
• They've learned not to take life too seriously.
• They speak about death in a fun way – one elderly woman always says to me 'I'll see you next week, if I'm not dead!'
• Behind tight-lipped crusty old people there are some really romantic stories – like in films.
• They talk to you!'

'Value each other. And value the differences between you and your friends. It's a great thing to have friendships across all age ranges and know old people as well as younger people.'
Mum

But I don't know anyone, and my grandparents aren't around
If you want to get to know someone in your church, why not ask your minister who would be a good person to get to know, and ask them to introduce you? Maybe you could drop in after school sometimes with a friend, or just talk to them on a Sunday at church for a while.

Guide to good friends!

I have loads of friends, but I don't have a best mate. I can't share what I really feel with my friends. How can I get a best mate?

that's exactly why they make such a good friend. Best friends should put your welfare above even your feelings. They will tell you things you may not want to hear in order to help you.

Do you need a best friend?
What makes a best friend?

It's perfectly OK to have a best mate – or not! Some people meet their soul mate at primary school and are inseparable for ever. And some don't.

One of the problems is that we think that our best friend should be somebody we really like, somebody with the same interests, someone we constantly hang out with and someone who thinks the same way. This isn't always the case! Sometimes your best mate is very different from you – and

Bible bit

Let's look at Jesus' friends. He had 12 close friends (disciples). But they were a real mixture. From a working class fisherman like Peter, to an upper class taxman like Matthew and a religious nut called Simon (known as a Zealot). Not forgetting Mary Magdalene – a prostitute. Jesus had a team around him. He didn't have one best friend, but he had 12 close friends with whom he shared good times, scary times, amazing times and bad times. Jesus cared for them, loved them but also often told them the truth and sometimes was even tough on them. He was the ultimate friend.

Some people don't have a best friend. The important thing is to have at least one or two good friends.

You can't choose a good friend. They evolve.

Sometimes you have a best friend without knowing it. Who's the person you trust? Who do you turn to when you feel stressed or in trouble? Who's the person who gives you advice? This is your best friend.

And distance doesn't matter as long as you can communicate and share stuff. A close friendship may only need regular chats on MSN or facebook with an occasional phone call, but you know that if you're in trouble and need help, you can call them ANY time, day or night and they will help you. Close friendship doesn't rely on how often you hang out together, but the respect and trust you have for one another. Respect and trust can never diminish because of distance. If it does, then the friendship was built on other things.

I don't have a best friend. What's wrong with me?
Nothing! Some people have a best friend, some don't. A good group of friends is what's important. That might be a whole crowd that you go everywhere with. Or you may have a load of friends from different places that don't even know each other. Someone at

---

What makes a good friend?
• Someone who doesn't expect you to turn into a clone of them.
• 'Someone I can trust and someone who trusts me.'
• Someone who tells you the truth.
• 'Someone who can take the mick out of me and have the mick taken out of them.'
• Someone who respects you.
• Someone who will stick up for you.
• 'Someone who says nice things to me to make me feel good about myself.'
• 'Someone who makes me laugh.'
• Someone who'll listen.

school, at church, at Scouts, from the camp you went on in the summer…

If you spend time with people in lots of different places, sooner or later you'll make some new friends. And if you have a good selection of friends, you'll get to know some of them better. Sooner or later you'll get some good friends! That might not be at school. School is almost the only place where people get thrown together and have NOTHING in common except for being the same age. And don't forget that sometimes we do make great friends who are absolutely, totally and completely different from us. More often, though, our best friends have a bit more in common with us – they like fishing, facebook, quizzes… or whatever it is we like! So if it's a bit tough at school, don't let that stop you from looking for new friends somewhere else.

So if you're looking to make some new friends, why not go to places where you'll meet people like you? You could try:
• going along to a church youth group
• looking on the web to see if there are any local Christian

Bible bit

And of course the number-one-best-mate-totally-loyal-right-behind-you-won't-ever-leave-you is Jesus Christ. Abraham was a man who trusted God through the total impossibility of beginning a great nation when he didn't think he could have children at all. You can read about him in Genesis 12–25. Life wasn't all easy going, but he stuck in there with God and the promises God made did happen. He was called 'God's friend' (James 2:23).

events which sound good – try www.yfc.co.uk
• joining a national young people's organisation with local groups – Urban Saints, Scouts, Guides, Boys' Brigade, Girls' Brigade
• doing some voluntary work
• going to the Christian Union at school
• going on a Christian holiday – Scripture Union and CPAS both run Christian holidays for people your age. Look at www.scriptureunion.org.uk/holidays or www.cpas.org.uk/ventures

• going to a national youth event like Soul Survivor (see www. soulsurvivor.com)

• asking your minister to find out if there are any youth events in your region

And back to your team…
Remember that one person can't fill every position! It puts a lot of pressure on them as you have so many expectations of them.

'Know who you can talk to. Nothing is ever so bad that you can't talk about it to someone else. Decide who you think is a good person to check your questions out with. Being well-informed is not smutty or an encouragement to have sex. Knowing what's what will help you make up your own mind. Opinions will often vary, and it's good to weigh up what others think.'

Youth worker

The people I like most are ones I meet on the web. So can you make a good friend on the web?
Great question! On the one hand, distance doesn't matter because of MSN, facebook and stuff. But how do you know someone's a good friend when you've never met them?

Firstly… meeting people online can be risky. Never share personal details with anyone you meet online. But if you find yourself on MSN with a friend of a friend, then there's little difference than being introduced to them at school or wherever. Or is there?

Certainly, the web gets rid of inhibitions and can help you build up your friendship base. But it's a different type of friendship where there is no human interaction. The response could just be from a computer that responds to anything you say! There might not be a person there at all! And if all your friends are on the internet, then it looks like your monitor might be your best mate. So then it's time to get out there and meet some live people to go with your virtual community!

Seriously – it's important to have a balance between being able to talk and mess about with friends online and actually to have a proper conversation. Research amongst employers says that the biggest weakness in young recruits is the ability to have a conversation about work with a potential customer. If most of your friendships are online, maybe you need to get out more!

But the most amazing news is that Jesus calls you his friend. Check out John 15:13–15. What will it take for you to be remembered as God's friend?

STOP How far is too far? ❓❓❓

My boyfriend and I have been going out for nearly a year. We're both Christians. We know that sex before marriage is wrong. We want to have sex. We're trying hard not to. But we're touching each other. How far is OK?

issues

What's OK and what's not?
Why isn't it OK?
Why do you want to be intimate?

It's been said that 'sex was created on the throne of God.' Sex is good. It is from God. It is meant to be great. So why doesn't anyone talk about it in church? It's as though sex is wrong and dirty. Sex is not dirty. Guess what? Your parents have had sex. Your grandparents have had sex. Even your vicar or pastor (if they are married) has had sex.

So if sex is so good, why all the stress on not doing it before you get married? Well, it's certainly not because God's a prude and doesn't approve of sex.

Sex is a gift, it's special

Imagine you're walking down a street. You see a total stranger. You walk up to them and give them your house keys, your bike, your mobile, your wallet/purse and your address. You tell them that you're going shopping for the next couple of hours. When you reach home you find that your house is a wreck. Your Wii has gone. So has your iPod. And clothes. And the TV…

How would you feel? Pretty gutted? Devastated? And pretty yuk inside. And you're unlikely to see the stranger again. They've taken everything.

If the stuff's insured, you'll be able to get more. But it's still been taken away. And that's exactly what happens when you have sex without being married. You have given the keys of your most intimate side, the most valuable part of yourself to a stranger. Maybe they don't feel like a stranger. But you don't know if things will work out with them or not. Even if they are drop dead gorgeous, you give them everything – the highest expression of love and commitment that you are capable of giving. Sex is the ultimate acceptance of a person. That's why in our law, a marriage isn't 'consummated' or confirmed until the couple have had sex.

Thousands of people have these experiences every day. By making love they are saying that they give themselves totally in 100% commitment to the person they are having sex with and that they ultimately accept that person, faults and all. Or do they? Outside a permanent relationship, by the next morning the person has usually left and you are on your own wondering whether you were any good or whether they really liked you or not. Did you please them? Did they laugh at your body?

(By the way, it's important to remember that whatever your friends say or do, it is against the law to have sex if you are under 16.)

'Girls, don't believe the lies boys tell you! Set your own values and have the courage to stick to them!'
Dad

'There's no insurance if they walk out on you a month down the line.'

So, just as you wouldn't give something valuable to a stranger, God doesn't want us to give the most valuable, intimate part of ourselves to someone who may not be around for ever. God's best for you is to give it to the person who will be honoured to receive you, and who will honour you and accept you.

'It has been said, that men overestimate the number of women they have slept with by 300%. If a guy tells you he's slept with someone, he may well be lying.'

But we love each other

If you love each other, then respect each other enough to wait. You don't know whether you will stay together. And if you have sex and split up later, how will you feel? And where is the line between having sex with the love of your life and sleeping around? Is it when you have had sex with the first love of your life? The second? The tenth?

The same goes for your body

Touching and exploring each other works in the same way. Back to the stranger with your house keys. Would you invite a complete stranger to come to your house and to look around? It's just tempting the stranger to come back and burgle your house. In the same way, touching leads to the temptation to have sex. Why would you do this with your body?

Even when you've known your boyfriend/girlfriend for a long time, there are other issues. There's the possibility of pregnancy; for girls, an increased risk of cervical cancer by having sex at a young age; and, once you have had sex, you take all the stuff from that relationship into every other relationship you have.

'The HIV message has been lost to teenagers. HIV is there. It's dangerous. And you can catch it from having unprotected sex.'

Bible bit

Sex is fun. And it's deep stuff. In the Bible (1 Corinthians 6:15,16) it says: 'Don't you know that your bodies are part of the body of Christ? Is it right for me to join part of the body of Christ to a prostitute? No, it isn't! Don't you know that a man who does that becomes part of her body? The Scriptures say, "The two of them will be like one person."'

So having sex with someone who is your life-long partner is about being with someone who will not reject you, or laugh at your body, but who wants to give everything of themselves to you. It's about being with someone who can give all that is valuable and precious to you and know that it will not be violated and wrecked. This shows us just how important sex is to God!

The fact is that you will have sexy feelings and thoughts. That's life! They're normal. Don't hide them or pretend they're not there. Your body changes and you become aware of sexual thoughts and feelings. And that's OK because they're natural. But it's because these feelings are natural and OK that you need to be careful about where you are and who you are with. So, being alone in a house or in your bedroom with your boy or girlfriend may not be the most sensible place to be! Being alone together, touching, will lead to sex – eventually. If you know with your head that you don't want sex before you're married, then don't put yourself in a place where your body might tell your brain to shut up!

'Think twice. Act once! Step back and think before you feel pressurised into becoming over-physical. Leaping into the sexual side of a relationship obliterates all the finer points of getting to know someone!'

GP

So what do I do with these feelings?

'Most blokes I know masturbate.'

'What else can you do? Wear an ice pack?!'

As you move through puberty you'll notice the changes in your body. You may start to explore your body; touching and feeling and even masturbating. Some things will feel very good! Many young people ask if masturbating is wrong. Well, masturbating itself isn't wrong or sinful. It's not mentioned in the Bible as being 'wrong'. One survey says that 95% of men and between 50 and 90% of women masturbate. It's safe to say that nearly everyone has masturbated at some time in their lives.

Bible bit

'Some of you say, "We can do anything we want to." But I tell you that not everything is good for us' (1 Corinthians 6:12). Could this relate to other areas of life – as well as masturbation?

In fact, there can be a positive side to masturbation. You may be ready for sexual experiences way before you are ready for marriage, commitment and parenthood, and masturbation can provide a natural safety valve for the sexual feelings that build up in you. It's a shame that masturbation often gets put into the unmentionable sin bin.

'You have to form your own opinion because no one talks about it.'

'Have you ever heard a Christian say that masturbation is OK? I've never even heard a Christian say "masturbation"!'

However, there are dangers in masturbation. Anything that becomes an obsession is dangerous, especially spiritually. Masturbation can easily become obsessive and out of control. Part of growing up into adulthood is to learn to control your sexual desires. Just as it's right to accept and honour sex as being good, we equally need to learn to control our sexual desires so that they don't control us. Do you like ice cream? If you do, a big bowl of choc chip brownie is fun every now and again. If you start to want it for breakfast, lunch and tea, and think about it most of the time in between, then you're becoming an ice cream obsessive! The same goes for masturbation. If you begin to get obsessed and need to masturbate really often, then it's time to talk to your youth leader, your parents or someone else in your team.

'Some people get hooked on routine. One lad even goes into the toilets at school.'

And porn?

'This picture opened on my computer by mistake and I quite liked it so sometimes I look at websites – but only when my parents are out.'

It's one thing looking at a book on your friend's parents' shelves, but you have absolutely no control over what opens on your computer. So don't. If you find it hard to stop, find a trusted adult and talk to them.

Help! I think I'm pregnant but I haven't had sex.

You can't get pregnant from kissing, or from kissing with all your clothes on. But if you take your underwear off and touch each other, it's unlikely, but it *is* possible to get pregnant. It's happened before. And you can also get sexually transmitted infections in the same way as with full sex.

Find an adult you trust unconditionally and get yourself a pregnancy test. You need someone who will listen and support you in this confusing time.

Did we do anything wrong?

There are Christians who say that anything short of full penetrative sex is OK. But the level of intimacy involved in touching and caressing is almost as identical as it is with having sex. Other Christians believe you shouldn't even kiss before marriage. You have to decide what's right from the Bible, your conscience, talking to God and knowing how far is far enough.

Back to great sex in marriage where there's plenty of time and opportunity to do whatever you like as long as it is respectful of both of you. We live in an instant

Bible bit

Your body is a temple of the Holy Spirit. (1 Corinthians 6:19). God's Spirit lives in you, so the whole of you belongs to God. That means your mind and your emotions. And also your penis, vagina, eyes and ears. So getting to know God and loving him as much as anyone else – and more – will help you in your relationships. Ask yourself the question: If I really love God, do I really want to do this?

society where we can get almost everything now. McDonalds, DVDs, your favourite TV show, instant communication with your mobile. And some people get what they demand immediately from their parents – designer clothes, gadgets and whatever else. Remember as a kid when you saved up for your dream toy? Every week you might have put a bit more money aside for it. And when you got it you knew how important it was (even if your parents subbed you the last few quid!). Instant toys often get chucked aside and left at the bottom of the toy cupboard. There is huge value in waiting for precious things. You are valuable and so is sex.

I know in my head what's right – what about the reality?
The statistics show the same levels of teenage sex for Christians as for those outside the church. Many people who have had sex young say that they would now like to wait until they are married. They've done it and they now see waiting is better. If you choose to wait, there will be times you have to have iron will! These pointers might help you:

• Talk to your girl/boyfriend and tell them that you want to wait until you are married (to someone!).

• Don't put yourself in a place where you are likely to be alone and get aroused – bedrooms when parents are out, isolated places outside etc.

• Know that you are very special and that it's an amazing gift to have sexual intimacy unlocked by the person who you'll spend the rest of your life with.

• Don't be ashamed of looking forward to great sex in marriage!

'The majority of teenagers are NOT having sex – whatever you may hear at school. You may think it's everyone, but even at 17, it's only about 30% of people.'
GP

Parents

Where have you been?

My mum reads my texts. I love her – but where do I draw the line?

It's great news that you get on well with your parents. But you're not going to want your mum to know everything. After all, if your friends wanted your mum to know what they were doing, they could text her! She loves you, and she's interested in your life (that's the good bit) but you're not getting much space!

'When I was 13 they were uptight, smothering, overprotective and really embarrassing.'

'Q Who's changed?
A We both have!'

Keep talking to her. Tell her that you like her to be interested, but that you prefer that she doesn't look at your texts. If it's email you're worried about, ask if you can set up a hotmail account. Then you'll have to trust that she'll respect that… or next time you'll have to padlock your phone in your pocket!

All this technology may be daunting for them. When asking for facebook or MSN, be patient and explain the facts to them. Suggest that they try to look at your account from another computer, to see how much of your personal information is on show to total strangers. Once they understand this, you'll stand more chance of making ground. And make sure you set your privacy settings high.

Dad wants to come to the pictures with me. What if anyone sees us?
One of the best gifts in the world is to have a good relationship

with your mum and dad. Don't let anyone knock it. So perhaps you don't want to do everything with them like you did when you were a kid, but enjoy a date with your dad! Under the pressure of school and exams, church, friends, sport, music, maybe a job even, parents get squeezed out. That's when it feels like you're only ever arguing. Have you done this? All that's said between you is: Tidy your room! Get up! Go to bed! (Funny, that one… maybe if you stayed in bed all day you wouldn't get the go to bed argument!) Give them some time.

You can have as much control about what happens with your parents as they do! Remember it's fine to laugh and have fun together… and even to cry. If your mum or dad aren't around much, or don't live with you, why not teach them how to text? You can be friends if you keep the communication going.

'My parents split up when I was 13. I can't be the only teenager who hated her mother.'

The world says that your friends are the most important people to listen to and be with. The Bible says respect your parents.

Bible bit

Even Jesus had a bit of banter with his mum. At the wedding in Cana, Mary tells Jesus that the wine's run out. 'Not now, Mum', says Jesus, but like many sons he did what she asked anyway! Check it out in John 2.

Friends are important. However out-of-date you might think your mum and dad are, they've lived a lot more life than you know! When you were a kid, if they shouted at you for getting too close to a fire, it was because they love you so much they didn't want you to be hurt. And nothing's changed! It's just that you probably argue a lot more – because although they tell you about the definite no-go areas like rollerblading on the motorway, they also have an opinion about drugs and alcohol and sex where other people say it's OK.

'And we were teenagers too – so maybe we regret some of the decisions we made and we want you to learn from that.'
Mum

'Children begin by loving their parents. As they grow older, they judge them. Sometimes they forgive them.'
Author unknown

However much you sometimes feel you'd like to, you can't change your mum and dad! You can only change yourself. When it all gets a bit hairy in your house, you are reacting to them and they are reacting to you, either to what you say or don't say. So when things are difficult, what can you do differently that will make life a bit more friendly?

'You may think we're pushy, but we want the best for you and we want you to succeed.'
Mum

'Pay attention to your father, and don't neglect your mother when she grows old.'
(Proverbs 23:22)

…and don't tell her she's old, either!

Online friends

MY BO FACE

Everyone else is on Twitter and facebook and my mum says I can't go on. They all see photos and I have to hope someone shares pictures on MSN.

Issues

Staying safe online
Cyberbullying

It's so annoying when everyone else is doing it. But she has a point because although your computer is in the safety of your house, the minute you put anything online, it's public. So whether it's Twitter, MySpace, facebook, MSN or whatever, there are some important things you need to remember even before you have that conversation with your mum.

Web 2.0 is moving so fast that within months you may be more likely to access the web on the move from your phone than from a PC in the kitchen! The world in your pocket... and you in the world's pocket

• It's only safe if you make it safe

• Only accept people as friends if you know them in real life – block them if you don't know them and delete them if you're uncomfortable

• People may not always be who they say they are – so your online friend who you're playing a game with could be anybody. Don't share any personal information at all – just use a nickname – and see if you can win that game!

• Only post – words or pictures – things that you'd be happy to have displayed on a billboard where you live. So don't tell everyone when you're going on holiday or share your address, mobile number or the date, time and location of your 13th birthday party! That's what email is for!

• If you put a picture online, any of your friends can save it and send it on. Is it OK for it to get into the hands of people who aren't your friends?

• Don't open anything from people you don't know and delete SPAM texts and emails straight away.

• If you wouldn't say it face to face to the person you're talking to, don't say it online. If you wouldn't shout it in the bus queue at school, don't say it on a message board or on your wall.

• Switch off Bluetooth if you're not using it – if you don't, other people can access your gadget and you may not realise it. Privacy settings are there to protect you so use them. Set them so that only friends can see your information and if you're on Twitter be especially careful to make the settings so that you have to approve followers – and then only people you know.

And if you're being bullied online or by text, ignore what's being said, keep the messages for evidence and go to one of the adults in your team who will help you find the way to report it.

 Peer pressure

My friends are drinking beer and smoking cannabis. They want me to do it too, but I don't want to. Will they still like me if I don't?

What is peer pressure?
How does it affect us?
How can we not be affected by it?
Is there anything good about peer pressure?

If one person at school asked you to drink a bottle of Magners at lunchtime, would you do it? If the whole class was drinking it and asked you to join in, would things be different?

It's far easier to say no to one person than it is to say no to five, ten or 20 people. Why? Because it's easier to go with the majority than it is to go against it.

When our friends or people around us are all doing something, we feel pressured to join in. And that's called peer pressure.

We don't want to be too different. Sure, it's OK to be the funny one in the group, or the serious one, or the tough one, or the 'nice' one. But you don't want to be the challenging one.

'If you deliberately do something different to the entire group, you get scared that they won't like you any more.'

Why are we affected by our peers/friends/people around us?
• We respect them.
• We fear them.
• We are intimidated by them.
• We want to please.
• We want to impress.
• We want to prove ourselves.

When you say to a group, 'Hey boys, I think you're wrong', it can be taken as a rejection of the whole group. You can be left out of the group, ignored, or in an extreme case, even attacked verbally or physically.

The danger of peer pressure
It's far easier to do something in a group than it is to do it alone. You can get far more boldness and strength from a group than you would by yourself. You can also find protection and acceptance in a peer group.

For some people, the peer group has become their family. On one estate in North London that I lived on, young people hung out in large groups because they felt safe and protected. They would do anything for each other.

It can almost be fun to do something wrong or illegal together. Maybe it's because it's harder to pin the blame on just one person. You almost share the blame – a quarter of the blame each, rather than full blame. It doesn't seem so serious, then.

'Individuals aren't strong but a group becomes strong.'

'My brother stole something just to be part of a gang.'

Peer pressure isn't only about bricks through windows or beer. It may just be the culture of always being rude to the teacher, picking on someone at school or everyone handing in homework late. Even with less extreme examples, the real danger is that you can become two different personalities: the 'you' in a group and the 'you' at home and on your own. You act differently depending where you are and who you're with. And this is all about how you feel about yourself (see the chapter about self-image). Is your identity in the people around you? Or are you comfortable with the person who watches TV or reads a book on their own?

> **'If you stand out from the crowd, you have to justify yourself. If you go with the flow, you don't.'**

How to cope with peer pressure

We've talked about 'What makes a good friend?' and learned that a friend tells the truth and respects you. That's what true friendship is about. In Galatians 2, Paul shows Peter that he is a true friend. He challenges Peter by telling him that what he is doing isn't good and is in fact wrong.

If you are really friends with the group that you're in, then you should tell them the truth. They may not like it at the time. They may be angry with you, or they may even not speak to you. But if they are truly your friends they will, eventually, respect you for it. If they don't, you will only

Bible bit

In Galatians 2:14, Peter gets himself into a bit of hot water because of peer pressure. Although Peter was a Jew, back in Acts 10 he met a Gentile called Cornelius and realised that God accepts non-Jews as well as Jews. Yet here in Galatians, Peter seems to change. He decides he can't eat with the Gentiles and goes and sits with all the Jews. Paul doesn't like this – and tells Peter exactly what he thinks. Peter was influenced by the Jews – he was put under pressure from the people around him and couldn't say no, even though it was something he no longer believed in!

have lost a group of friends who were willing to try and force you to do things that you didn't want to do. Remember that the majority isn't always right!

So is peer pressure bad news all the time?

Actually, peer pressure isn't always a bad thing. Peer pressure can be good and it can have loads of benefits. If you have a group of friends who

Bible bit

The Ultimate Peer Group were, of course, the 12 disciples. They hung out together for three years. They travelled, ate, slept, walked, talked and did amazing things together. They got on each other's nerves and argued. In Luke 9:46 they argue over which one of them is the greatest, and in Mark 10:35 James and John ask Jesus if they can have the places of honour in heaven next to him. When the other disciples find out, they get a bit narked! In the end, as Jesus goes to the cross, Peter says he doesn't know him at all. Some friend! But he's still accepted in the group. Sometimes life is tough. Good friends will accept that. The disciples grew in every way. And from 12 believers, we now have a world where over 1 billion people follow Jesus – WHAT AN AMAZING PEER GROUP!

respect you, accept you and are honest with you, then you have the makings of a group that will help you grow; mentally, physically, spiritually and emotionally. They will give you confidence and encourage you.

That's why it's important to have Christian friends. There may be a great group in your church – or you may need to go to youth events locally to meet up with people. Or try a summer camp (www.scriptureunion.org.uk/holidays) or an event like Soul Survivor (www.soulsurvivor.com) and get the group vibes when you get home through texts and messenger. You'll be able to support each other… and in the same way you might tell a friend they're out of order, they can tell you too!

So within a good peer group, you will learn to cope with difficult situations, relationships and emotions in and amongst the group. You will learn to solve problems, develop social skills and understand personalities.

Hang on – what about alcohol and cannabis, then?

Pressure from friends and people around often comes about things that you're not really sure about. Shall I have my belly button pierced? What about a tattoo? Everyone else is doing it. 'Go on – try it…' it might be a bottle of beer or a puff of a cigarette or cannabis.

'Know what you think. Reading this sort of book is good – it helps you to think through what you think about relationships. It's good to think things through away from more risky situations. Once peer pressure, alcohol, or a persuasive or perhaps manipulative person take over, it's more difficult to think clearly. If you know what you think and have thought through in advance how you would like to respond or act in a certain situation, it's more likely to happen that way. It's not guaranteed, but it helps.'
Youth worker

Drugs and alcohol are all around you. No one can stop you taking drugs or drinking alcohol apart from you. And you have to choose. What do we believe? Jesus never broke the law of the land. Sure, he may have broken lots of the religious laws which were made up by men of the day, but he never broke God's law, or the Roman law which ruled at the time. He paid his taxes (Mark 12:15–17) and even Pilate could find no wrong in him! Paul says that we have to do what the government tells us to do because they have been put there by God (Romans 13:1–10).

Drinking under-age or taking drugs is simply against the law. Whether it should be against the law is irrelevant. If Jesus himself didn't break a law of the land, do we have the authority to break a law, regardless of whether we think the law is right? Colossians 3:23 says that we should do everything as if we're doing it for Jesus himself. Is drinking under the legal age honouring Jesus? Is taking an illegal drug honouring to Jesus?

What about the facts?
• 40% of 14- to 16-year-olds have experimented with illegal drugs. (From CARE's article 'Living in A Drug Taking Society')

• 25% of 11- to 14-year-olds have tried illegal drugs.

• 1% of 11-year-olds have at least one drink in a week.

• 31% of 15-year-olds have at least one drink in a week. (From the National Statistics website)

Addicts didn't plan to be addicts. They had one drink or drag or pill… and then another and suddenly they're hooked and instead of them being in control, the substance is in control. That's a choice they made.

'Did your Mum really say you shouldn't take drugs? Surely nothing will happen.' Sounds very 21st century. But take a look in the Bible – it's all been said before. The serpent in the Garden of Eden says to Eve, 'Did God really say, "You must not eat from any tree in the garden?"… You will not surely die!' She ate one piece of fruit – and the relationship between God and humans was changed for ever.

Only you can decide. Choices will be put in front of you by friends, acquaintances or even family. And the choice is yours. People will tell you that it won't hurt, it'll be fun and if you don't have a go you're a wuss. At the end of the day, you still have a choice.

Help! I'm really fed up. Mum and Dad don't like me spending too much money on clothes. But I feel a real idiot if I don't. And I've got spots.

Does how I look matter? **What** is it that makes me who I am?

Q Why does everyone in magazines always look perfect? A They don't! All their spots have been airbrushed out!

Have a look at http://www.youtube.com/watch?v=hibyAJO SW8U&feature=fvw

Everywhere you look there are perfect images of people – on TV, on the posters in your bedroom and in magazines. We see perfect people wearing perfect clothes with perfect bodies. And the result is that:

• You try and look like that. You buy the clothes and have the haircut.

• You suddenly realise that you will never achieve that level of 'perfect'. You might never be that thin, or that big, or that tall, and so you feel rubbish.

But life's not actually like that! And even for the rich and famous, money can't buy

Bible bit

Did you know that you have an image that is out of this world? The Bible tells you that you are 'created to be like God' (Genesis 1:27). Your image is based on the God who created you. It also says in Psalm 139:13 that God knitted you together inside your mother's body. God made you special because there is only one of you in the whole world. You are purposely made with a purpose. Why tamper with it?

everything. It's interesting that so many people with fame, good looks, loads of money and great bodies get so depressed and end up on drugs or addicted to alcohol. You only need to look on the front cover of *OK* and *Hello*. That's enough to drive anyone nuts! Don't let other people or other things determine the person you are.

> 'People are people. Not superhuman. Whoever you are talking to and whoever's on your team has usually been through the things you've been struggling with. Many teachers will have been told off at school. And some will have been bullied.'
> **Teacher**

Everyone else has designer labels on their clothes
You are who you are. Clothes and make-up and hair wax won't change that. It's great to look good… but trying to look like Matt Damon or Vanessa Hudgens will only make you unhappy. Because if you're anything like me and Andy, you'll never succeed!!

Without them I don't feel good
Great clothes are fun. They look fab if that style suits you, but you are more than your clothes! Our confidence comes from the inside. Bodies and clothes are just the packaging. It's good to be in a smart package, but it's the contents that really matter.

> 'Being a sex symbol has to do with an attitude, not looks. Most men think it's looks; most women know otherwise.'
> **Kathleen Turner**

You need to work on the inside part of you with as much effort as you work on the outside.

What about everyone else? What about what they think?
It doesn't help much when someone says to you, 'It doesn't matter what other people think.' Facing a crowd of friends or classmates in Nike footwear when you're wearing trainers off the market can be tough. However, if you're sure of who you are yourself – and who you are as a great child of God – it doesn't matter if you're wearing Versace or Own Brand. At some point you need to decide who is going to define who you are – other people (in which case

you will always be at the mercy of their whims) or God, who thinks you are fantastic and accepts you for who you are.

'What matters is not your outer appearance – the styling of your hair, the jewellery you wear, the cut of your clothes – but your inner disposition. Cultivate inner beauty, the gentle, gracious kind that God delights in.' 1 Peter 3:4 (*The Message*)

'Remember that you have a tremendous amount of really good qualities. Be positive about yourself!'
Dad

'Know who you are. You're a unique individual designed by God. You may not always feel this way when you're confronted with the things about yourself you don't like or would like to change. Think about the things about yourself you'd like to keep – go on. Everyone can think of a couple of things!'
Youth worker

10 steps to a beautiful inside:
1 Know where you fit in history.
2 Remember that God has plans for you.
3 Spend as much time making over who you are as you do what you look like.
4 Listen to God.
5 Listen to yourself.
6 Ditch the dirt – say sorry to other people when you need to (and not only when you want to).
7 Have a good wash: tell God about the bits you don't like and the bits that you're ashamed of.
8 Find friends who have beautiful insides!
9 Smile every day!
10 Grow some fruit. Nope, not in your garden – look in Galatians 5:22.

Strip away all your clothes, make-up and hair straighteners and what are you left with (apart from being naked!)?

'I need people to tell me I'm OK to feel OK.'

And as for the spots...
Bodies change! Did you know that it's a medical fact that no part of your body is older than seven years? Your body is constantly changing. Your skin, your hair, your liver and all kinds of bits are continually being renewed! As you go from 11 to 18, all kinds of things happen – hairy bits, spots and all that. Sorry to not have any miracle cures, but you will come out at the other end – and changes like that are a normal part of life. And if it's stressing you out, see the doc!

Confidential!
There are two types of confidence: absolute unshakeable confidence in who you are, and confidence in what you do. It's far easier to have confidence in what you do than in who you are. Your ability in computers, as a sports person, a dancer or in your studies is measurable. You can't argue with an A star. Yet we feel differently when it comes to measuring ourselves and who we are.

Mohammed Ali, one of the greatest boxers in history, had lots of confidence in his ability: 'I am the greatest. I said that even before I knew I was. Don't tell me I can't do something. Don't tell me it's impossible. Don't tell me I'm not the greatest. I'm the double greatest.'

What makes me confident?
1 When someone says something positive about me.
2 Friends that accept me.
3 Knowing I'm good at something.
4 Feeling relaxed where I am.
5 When my hair goes right and stays where I put it.
6 Enjoying myself.
7 Hormones!
8 A good day – even when bad things happen.
9 Not smelling gross.
10 Clothes.

But that's confidence in yourself, or even arrogance. God-confidence is something much more amazing. God-confidence gives us unshakeable confidence in who we are. It's like the roots of a tree. When they go deep into the ground, even a gale will leave the tree standing.

'They are like trees growing beside a stream, trees that produce fruit in season and always have leaves.'
Psalm 1:3

'Never sell yourself short. Never feel that other people are always better than you – you are worth a lot. Academic work isn't the be-all and end-all. If you've messed up, don't stress about it. There's always a chance to have another go. Don't judge yourself against exam results and how clever other people might be – that's just a tiny bit of who you are.'
Teacher

Know God
Spend time listening to God and reading what he has to say about you! Know that he loves you.

Listen to the good stuff
People will always say stuff about you. Some will be great. Some won't. Listen to the good stuff. Get someone in your team who will tell you you're doing great (and maybe do a bit of challenging when you're not!). It may be your mum or dad, or even someone you don't know particularly well. Make sure you have this position covered! Find a leader, a teacher or a friend who will help you feel confident in yourself.

Have good friends first
Get some good friends around you – of both sexes. Caring, loving friends are more valuable to you as a person than romance. They can be loyal and fun and good for your self-image!

Celebrate
When things have gone well, remember to celebrate. You did a great thing. And remember to thank God, too!

Z Z Z Z Sleepovers

When I go for a sleepover at my mate's, we have to share a double bed as that's all there is. Is it OK?

issues

Is it OK?
Will people think I'm gay?
If I share a bed will it make me gay?
What about overnight parties?

Sleepovers! The fact is that most people in the UK don't have a mansion with miles of carpet in the bedroom so that loads of people can sleep over really easily. More likely on a sleepover you'll be crammed into the little space there is. If your mate has a double bed and the choice is bed or floor, what will you choose?

There's nothing wrong with sharing a bed on a sleepover. In Africa, people sleep far more than two to a bed! Same sex

sleepovers are fine. And if you need somewhere to kip, a double bed is as good as any!

'I've done it when there aren't enough duvets for people...'

WARNING SIGN: If you have any bad feelings about it, stick with the floor! And if you have any sexual feelings about it, get out!

What about a multi-sex sleepover?

…which must mean girls and boys! What do you need to think about? Check out:
• Are parents going to be there?
• How well do you know the other people who are going?
• Do you trust them?
• Do you know who you'll be sharing a room with?
• Is there anyone there who you fancy? Or who fancies you?

If there will be adults in the house and you know and trust the people going, then this could be totally harmless. If it's going to turn into a night of getting into other people's sleeping bags, then you may decide that will compromise the beliefs and values you have.

Some parents may have a problem with two boys sharing a bed. For centuries in Western culture, it's been said that men shouldn't have any physical contact. Until the twentieth century, homosexuality was an offence and you could be sent to prison for being gay. It has been a taboo.

But… sharing a bed with your mate won't make you gay! Neither does having sport's number one physical pseudo cuddle… a rugby scrum! If you start having sexual feelings about a same sex friend, then it's not such a good idea to share a bed. You need to be honest with yourself that it's happening. It's not odd or unusual to have a crush on or to be attracted to a same sex friend. But again, that doesn't make you gay. Your body is changing. Physical things happen – boys can get erections, girls can get aroused – whether you're sharing a bed or watching a film or minding your own business!

It's easy to get confused between affection and physical attraction and as a teenager you may not even feel particularly

Bible bit

Jesus and his disciples lived together for three years. They didn't go home at night, or for weekends. They travelled and also sleptover together. They were just friends.

attracted to anyone. Or you may feel attracted to everyone!

Because your emotions and hormones are up and down, any decision about your sexuality needs to wait until you are older. If you have had a physical encounter with someone of the same sex, don't panic! Be friends. Now is not the time to have a sexual relationship with anyone. If you're concerned that you're thinking a lot about same sex relationships, find a trusted member of your team and talk to them. It doesn't mean you're gay. And remember that we can pray about everything! There is absolutely nothing that God doesn't know about you! No room for surprises or shock.

So, if you're sharing a bed on a sleepover because you're totally shattered and looking for a kip – then do it! If you're looking to play games, then forget it!

Snogging is fun! Is it wrong?

Feelings
Results of snogging
How close do you get?

There's a Chinese proverb that says that a journey of a thousand miles begins with one step. At the beginning, the journey is fun. So where are you going? Where are you thinking you might end up?

Yes, snogging can be fun! Why are you doing it? Is it…
A Market research for a breath freshener?
B Just for fun?
C Because it turns you on?
D Because you're going out with the person?
Well, unless your Saturday job is as a market researcher, the answer should be D!

A long time ago, people used to greet one another with a handshake. Now that seems really old-fashioned except in some cultures. The next physical greeting was the peck on the cheek. The air kiss! Turn your head and you get a face full of chin! Now it can even be

Get physical!
• We are sexual people.
• Even innocent touches when someone brushes past can feel nice.
• Any kind of touching can feel good (unless it's abuse).
• Snogging is intimate contact – touching lips and tongues is more intimate than shaking hands!
• When you kiss you begin to open up feelings which you may not be able to control.

acceptable to greet people with a kiss on the lips. On the other hand, kissing is very intimate – especially if it's all tongues and slobber! When you kiss, physical changes happen in your body as it prepares for sex.

If you snog with a mate, just for fun, is that OK?
Just because it's all done openly doesn't mean it's right! Especially if it's not even the beginning of a relationship. You're joining your bodies together. Put that way, is that really what you want to do? Would you go skinny-dipping with a mate of the opposite sex? Probably no way!

'My first kiss was with someone I didn't fancy. I met him after school and snogged his face off.'

The big question is: what's appropriate? Snogging in a relationship is OK, but like we've said before, decide how far it's OK to go… and make sure that you don't snog in your bedroom with the door closed (or anywhere else where you're on your own!) when you might be tempted to go one step too far.

Girls often get much more of a thrill from snogging than blokes. In romantic stories on TV and in mags, if it's the girl's point of view, you get atmosphere and music as their heads move closely together and he touches her lips… And for lads, snogging often isn't the end. They get aroused much more quickly than girls and the idea of sex suddenly becomes rather physical! This can cause problems of its own, because you have to really know when

Bible bit

Proverbs 7:6–23 is one of those bits of the Bible that gets straight to the point! A young bloke didn't have much common sense. An immoral woman came up to him and kissed him and then she entices him back to her house for you-know-what. The thing is, he should have said, 'No way!', but instead he follows her 'like an ox on the way to be slaughtered'. From a kiss, you can lead yourself down a path that you might regret in the future. Use your common sense. Yes, snogging can be fun, but it can also be the beginning of something that you don't want to do!

to stop if your body is shouting 'Get on with it!'

Back to the line. Where is it? In Islam, women are covered so you can't see any of their body, and it is (meant to be) forbidden for boys and girls to even touch before marriage. That's a very firm line. For Christians, the Bible doesn't explicitly say 'Don't snog Sam Smith!' or give step-by-step instructions about what's OK and what's not. It just gives guidelines. In a way you then have to make your own decisions. How close do you go to the edge?

Many young people who have stepped up to the line and have ended up having sex wish they hadn't and are now much more sure of what is and isn't OK for them. But you can't press the delete button on what's happened in the past, even though we are forgiven people. So it's important to decide what you think is OK. Talk about it with your girl/boyfriend and stick to it. And if you're not in – or on the way into – a relationship, what are you snogging for?

'In our school common room there's a sign saying "No heavy petting".'

'I don't like it to get too heavy or it might escalate.'

The REAL best friend

If you could list ten people who you would like to be your friend, I wonder who would be on your list. Imagine having Zac Efron as a mate, or Cheryl Cole as a shopping pal (expensive!). It would be great to have such a famous and powerful figure as your friend. You would get respect, probably get great presents and you would tell everyone you met that you were friends with Zac Efron or Cheryl Cole.

Yet you have a friend who makes Zac Efron and Cheryl Cole look totally second best. In fact, he is your best friend, and has remained your best friend even though you may have ignored him, treated him badly, stormed off or even ditched him a few times.

In terms of influence, your best friend has no equal. There is no one more powerful, more important or more influential. And this best friend of yours is totally committed to you.

OK, you've probably twigged that we're talking about Jesus.

Yet do we really see Jesus as our friend? In John 15:14,15 Jesus says that he no longer calls us servants but friends. When you can get your head around what that means for you, it could change your life.

God created the world. He's totally awesome. We could view God as someone to be afraid of, always trying to be good enough to meet his expectations and feeling as though we are cowering in the corner. If that's how you acted when your friends came round, people would think your friends intimidate you. They would think that you were not really friends. That's because friendship is not based on fear.

God sent his Son, Jesus, to live in our world. And it's Jesus who helps us to see God as a friend – as someone who just loves spending time with you, who longs to do things for you, who wants you to walk with him in the adventure of life and who wants you to let him show you how life should be lived.

As your friend, Jesus has made you some promises. Promises that he will never break. Imagine Jesus is speaking to you:

'I promise I will never leave you. I will keep you safe from evil. You'll never die because you will live for ever with me in heaven. I will care for you. Nothing at all can separate you from my love. No one at all can snatch you away from my hand. And when you talk to me, I'll listen to you.'

These are just a few of the amazing promises personally given to you, because you are a friend of Jesus. When you're feeling down, when you're alone, when you feel rejected by others, Jesus will always be there. He will never fail you. He needs to be the captain of your team.

(Check out the promises in Matthew 6:30; Matthew 21:22; Matthew 28:20; John 3:16; John 10:28,29; John 17:15; Romans 8:39)

What do you want your parents to know?

I was out really late last night with my friend. My parents want to know what we were doing. What do I tell them?

What should you tell your parents?
Why do your parents get angry?
Who's in your team?
Why should your parents trust you?

Hey! What's the problem?

'It makes a big difference if your parents are still together or not. My mum's on her own and she doesn't care because she's looking for a partner of her own.'

There are two kinds of parents: those who want to know everything and those who want to know nothing! You can either feel that your parents are constantly interfering, or that they don't care at all what you're doing. What's the in-between? Well, it should be careful concern with a dash of trust, topped with a nice dollop of understanding. And this works BOTH ways!

'My parents are responsible for me.'

Trust, honesty and respect have to come from both your parents and from you! Most families have a 'Parent/Teenager Power Struggle.' Sound familiar? Your parents do have authority over you, but the way in which they relate to you may have something to do with the way their parents treated them. Parents can sometimes impose something on you simply by saying, 'I'm older than you and I know better', regardless of whether they're right or wrong. This isn't helpful. A parent/teenager relationship must operate on mutual trust, honesty and respect. It should be a friendship. And this may mean you rebuking or telling off parents for their mistakes, and parents accepting the telling off and apologising!

'Respect your father and your mother… Parents, don't be hard on your children…'
(Exodus 20:12; Colossians 3:21)

'You can never win with your parents because they say they're older than you and they know better.'

'Know we all make mistakes. Sometimes you'll miss the mark. Find a way to sort it out and try to move on – don't be too hard on yourself. Accept forgiveness from God, forgive yourself and forgive others who are involved too. And remember that no adult has got it right with every relationship!'
Youth worker

'What I want my parents to know depends on their agenda!'

What should I be telling them, then?

'Mum always knows where I've been and what I've done! She only asks me to see if I'm lying!'

You're you! As you move from being a child to being an adult, it's not always appropriate to tell your parents everything. After all, they don't tell you everything. And that's right. But too often they demand everything from you! Your parents don't have a right to know everything about you, just as you don't have a right to know everything about them. True relationships don't exist on rights. Your parents love you very much. They may not realise how demanding they are being. Communicate with them – and respect their feelings.

'Parents have a right to know that you're safe, but not to know everything.'

'When I was nine, I told my mum that a boy had asked me out. She laughed in my face. I never told her about boys again until I was 16.'

What is important is that you have a trusted adult(s) to whom you can tell everything if you want to. This can be a tricky area. Your parents may feel upset that you might prefer to talk to someone outside the family rather than tell them, especially if it's to do with something personal or intimate. You may need to help your parents understand this. It's not that you don't love or need them, but that there are some things that are helpful to talk about with someone who is not related or emotionally involved with you. Your parents almost certainly have friends like these themselves.

You may already know someone you could talk to. If not, who might it be? Someone who's around (or is excellent at texting!) and with whom you feel safe. You'll feel much more comfortable if they don't demand to know everything – but you may need to answer a few direct questions!

'I would lie to my parents, especially if I was going out drinking.'

Having an adult you can talk to doesn't give you a licence to lie to your parents. That's wrong, just as it's wrong for your parents to lie to you. Relationships and friendships can only exist on trust, honesty and respect. If you've done something wrong, or are in trouble, hiding it is the worst thing you can do. If you've picked your team well, the person you talk with will help you to deal with it, and that may mean telling your parents.

Why might M&D have been so furious?

'If you come home late, parents automatically assume you've been drinking or snogging or more – no matter how much you said you were just talking. It's a lack of trust on their part.'

'It reflects on your parents if they have to ask you what you were doing, because it shows they don't trust you.'

There's a reason why most mums and dads get furious if you do something wrong or come home way after midnight. Chances are they were dead worried about you and it's spilled out into 'What on earth do you think you were up to last night?' Often, instead of showing the worry that they feel, parents can get heavy-handed instead. Their love, concern and worry for you pours out in commands. Why not just ask them, 'What's the problem? Were you worried about me?' And if they say yes, you know why they are saying what they are saying to you. And if this is the case, then maybe it's your turn to be reasonable! Apologise for worrying them. Tell them that you'll phone next time. Recognise that your parents need to know you're safe.

'When you start to do new things by yourself, we're frightened. We've been your protector and guide and been around to stop dangerous things happening to you... and suddenly you begin to get out on your own. It's difficult.'
Mum

'I'll stand with you and help you say no in places where you want to be strong, but it's tough. I'll be the horrible parent who'll check up on you and tell you to be home by whenever. But I'll be reasonable too. You'll say your friends don't have rules like these, but they'll wish they did.'
Dad

Your parents have spent the last however many years bringing you up, teaching you to clean your teeth, cross the road and tell the difference between right and wrong. At some point they'll have to trust that they've done a good job. If there's nothing for them to be worried about, you can tell them to trust all the great stuff they've put into you. Eventually you'll leave home if, for instance, you go to university or get a job in another town. In a matter of weeks you can go from clear rules, where you have to be home at ten o'clock, to a place with no boundaries at all when you can come home when you want to.

Part of your job is to help educate your parents. One of

Bible bit

In Colossians 3:20,21 it says that children should obey their parents. But it also says, 'Parents, don't be hard on your children'! The Bible spells it out loud and clear – your relationship with your parents is a two-way thing. Often there's a power struggle going on in the home. And too often, parents exercise their authority even when they shouldn't – which irritates their children. A parent/child relationship has always meant to operate on a mutual understanding of respect, honour and trust. A parent's role can be seen as one of stewardship. God has placed a child he has created into the stewardship of parent/s, so they can love the child, and teach him or her the ways of God. And our old friend 1 Corinthians 13 shows us the basic elements of any relationship or friendship. Love requires an immense amount of trust.

the young people we spoke to said that when you are young, children are like empty computer shells. Parents, who are the top of the range models, begin to install your software: behaviour, ethics, morals etc. The problem is that very soon, the older computer becomes outdated. Its memory capacity doesn't match the new model. As the newer computer grows, the older computer is no longer compatible with it. The only option for the old computer is to have a memory upgrade – change its existing package for a new one!!

Just as an old computer can no longer be networked or communicate with a newer computer without an upgrade, so parents need to upgrade their understanding in order to be networked. And that job falls on your shoulders!

'We know we often don't get it right in your eyes. Remember that this is our first time having a 14-year-old, too. Sometimes we'll get it wrong.'

Mum

Friends First team

Rewind...

Let's go back to the beginning. If your life is a sports match, who else is in your team?

How has your team changed since you began dipping into *Friends First*?

Who are the people in your life who bring in the sponsorship (and the social life and the excitement)?

_____

_____

_____

_____

Which are the positions you need to fill – like the goalie and the centre half (having fun friend, friend to be miserable with, friend to learn about God with etc.)? And who fills them?

Good friends positions

Having fun friend

_____

'What's the homework?' friend?

_____

'Help me! I need some wisdom' friend

_____

'Another look on life' older person friend

_____

Best friend

_____

_____

_____

'I'd want:
- **a best friend to chill with**
- **a best friend who's honest with me**
- **a best friend who mucks up sometimes**
- **friends who are there all the time**
- **some supporters**
  – parents, but sometimes they're like the coach and a bit critical
- **an experienced friend – captain**
- **a substitute (very important)'**

And who are the people who just have to be in your team no matter what part they fill?

‾‾‾‾‾‾‾‾‾‾‾‾‾‾‾‾‾‾‾‾

‾‾‾‾‾‾‾‾‾‾‾‾‾‾‾‾‾‾‾‾

‾‾‾‾‾‾‾‾‾‾‾‾‾‾‾‾‾‾‾‾

‾‾‾‾‾‾‾‾‾‾‾‾‾‾‾‾‾‾‾‾

‾‾‾‾‾‾‾‾‾‾‾‾‾‾‾‾‾‾‾‾

'Your family doctor is a good person to have in your team. They won't say ANYTHING to your mum and dad (they're not allowed to) and you can go to see them on your own. If you're at all worried or concerned and want to see your doctor, just phone and make an appointment.'
GP

Like we said right at the start, the key to great friendships is to have a good team around you. Is Jesus in your team? And what's his position?

'I have called you friends.'
Jesus Christ

Index

the way

- **Read the Bible**

- **Get to know God better**

- **Find out more about Jesus**

SUbmerge
A Bible reading guide for you – the way you want it